Journey of a Gentle Southern Man

Reflections from the Road

Dust cover illustration by Wimberley Rader

Library of Congress Card Number 99-65742

ISBN 1-892298-15-5

Printed in the United States of America

Journey of a Gentle Southern Man

Reflections from the Road

Jackie K. Cooper (signature)

Jackie K. Cooper

ABIQUE
Plano, Texas
For big discounts on our books
http://members.xoom.com/abique

About the Author

Jackie K Cooper was born in Clinton, South Carolina. During his journey he has been a lawyer, a personellist, a movie critic, a TV personality, and an after dinner speaker. He has two sons and now lives with his wife Terry in Perry, Georgia where he continues his journey one day at a time.

Dedicated to my mother, Virginia, who guides my life
and
To my wife, Terry, who is the perfect partner for my journey

Table of Contents

Foreword by Larry Mobley

Different readers will claim different favorites among Jackie K. Cooper's first collection of essays, but for me the most entertaining and revealing are those that seek connections between Perry, Georgia of the late 1980's and Clinton, South Carolina of the 1950's. This movement in time and place occurs frequently enough to constitute the characteristic pattern and theme of the collection as a whole. As Jackie K. Cooper journeys from Perry to Clinton and back, he dramatizes and celebrates the enduring values of love, friendship, and community that for this gentle, Southern man make life meaningful.

Repeatedly, present events are enriched by the author's revelations of their symbolic links to the past. His great delight in opening the daily mail, for example, derives from memories of that "good man" J. D. McKee, the mailman in Clinton who spoke with the voice of God and whose daily offerings so excited the six year old boy that he would leave the house and look up the street every afternoon at one o'clock. In another essay the simple observation of his son's sleeping while the author drives the two of them to the movies triggers memories of the "absolute security and trust" the author knew as a child when he slept in the car driven by his father. His discovery that the wonder and love generated in that place has been replicated in this place gives to many of these essays a dominant tone of gratitude. It's no wonder that Jackie K. Cooper describes the year's of 1986-1988 as his best.

Jackie K Cooper insists on the value of the past, but he does not return to it out of nostalgia. Some of these were good old days, but some of them were not. The death of his mother when he was fourteen serves as a constant reminder that his was a vulnerable world subject to the most profound losses. Moreover, as the essay on his childhood friend Hollis shows, he knows full well the present disappointment of those who idealize their pasts as the best times in their lives.

Another way by which the author avoids sentimentalizing the past is with his abundant sense of humor. Always ready to laugh, especially at himself, the author shares with us many episodes which show how adherence to tradition makes fools of us all. His friend Nancy's advice to all brides to eat as much as they can before their weddings is one example, and his admission to being addicted to electric fans is another. My favorite is his account of his own wedding day when at great price he subdued his nervous perspiration and met his bride at the altar with an appropriately dry face.

Without sentimentalizing his childhood, Jackie K Cooper reminds us that not only can we go home again but at times we must do so. Unless we revisit, however imaginatively, our own Clintons, too much of who we were and what we have become remains buried. We will hardly be able to account for our own motives, and we will not begin to understand the hurts and hopes of our children. Thanks to Jackie K Cooper, at least one Clinton is only a few pages away.

Larry Mobley
Professor of English
Macon University

Prologue

Every life is a journey. Some are more involved than others with a variety of side trips taken along the way, while others appear to move in a straight line toward some singular goal. Mine has been a little of both.

In some ways it has been like a marathon race, not because of the competition but because of the speed in which it has passed. Also there were so many of us at the start and now some are dropping out.

For the first fourteen years of my life I was in a state of bliss. Honestly, I had the most idealistic life anyone could have. I had loving parents, a comfortable home, great friends, and rose-colored glasses stuck on my face that made me happy about everything.

My mother told me I should be thankful for these blessings and that I should adapt my life to reflect these gifts of goodness I received. She was raising me to be a southern gentleman she said with the emphasis on "gentle." She would quote a phrase to me she had heard, "Only a person who is strong can afford to be gentle." She didn't know where it originated, and neither do I, but I have adapted that as a mantra for my life.

Margaret Virginia Kershaw Cooper died when I was fourteen, and her death was the kickoff to my journey. From that point on life was harder, and from that point on I was searching for the stability she had given me. It took me years to find it, and by then I was looking for other avenues of adventure to pursue along my way.

This book takes a look at some of the observations I have made on my trek. The chapters entitled "The View From Routes 86, 87 and 88" refer to the years of 1986, 87 and 88. In the film "The Way We Were" the characters played by Bradford Dillman and Robert Redford test each other by asking the name of best movie, best food, etc. In one scene they ask about the best years and several are named. Well, in my life these years of 86-88 were three of the best. So I have included some of my viewpoints from this era.

This is a book to be read with care and deliberation. It isn't a page-turner in that you have to rush to see what is happening next. The main character is there at the start, and I guarantee is there at the end.

So digest this book slowly. Put it on your night stand and read a few chapters each night. Read it "gently."

The road of life stretches out before us. Read on and learn how one (hopefully) gentle southern man has lived his.

Reflections from Route 86

Route 86 reflects my thoughts from the year 1986. This was the year I first began to write down my thoughts about my life and how I had come to be where I was on my journey. This was a time when I had finally gotten married, had two sons, a cat named Fluff, and felt as blissfully happy as possible. To determine how I had reached that state, I looked back at my life, especially my growing up time in Clinton, South Carolina. There I had the best of times and the worst of times. Read on and you can see which were which.

There Is Life After High School

A few weeks ago I saw a movie about a high school kid who worried the girls wouldn't like him because he wasn't a football star. Now that doesn't sound like much of a basis for a movie, but what impressed me is that kids are still worrying about the same things I worried about when I was in high school back in the 50s.

At first glance, it would appear I had everything going for me in high school. I was smart, good-looking, friendly, had enough money if not rich and got along with everyone. Plus I had the best-looking girlfriend at Clinton High.

But my life was a wreck. I did not have a block "C." To get one of those you had to be good at sports or be a cheerleader, and this was in the days before boys were cheerleaders. My girlfriend was a cheerleader, and she had her own block "C."

This lack of a letter was like a black cloud hanging over my head. I was a failure, a wimp, a sissy, a nerd. How could sweet Dorothy love me when I didn't even have a letter sweater to give her? Even though she swore it didn't matter, I knew in her heart she was disappointed.

So what was I to do? I hated sports. Hated getting tired. Hated getting hit. Hated to sweat. I liked movies, books, records, concerts and generally just being physically lazy. Life on the athletic field was not something I would seek. So I spent my days as a senior in a funk. Too stupid to see beyond my limited view and too lazy to do anything about it.

It came time for the senior superlatives to be elected. My friends and I being a shrewd group decided to spread the word as to which one we each wanted and not leave the choice or chance to fate. Which would I campaign for, that was a problem. "Most popular" was out as that required a letter in sports, I assumed.

The same was usually true of "best personality." I had lumped "best all-round" in that same category. "Most talented" or "most intelligent" would cinch my fate as Nerd of the Year, so I didn't want those. I would have liked to have been named "best looking," but my ego was not quite high enough to campaign for that one.

So I settled on "most likely to succeed." That sounded good, solid and non-wimpish. I'd go for it. I passed the word to my group of friends and took their goals and spread them around.

The first day we voted for "most popular." My friends and I had our candidate for "most popular" girl, but the boy to be named was up for grabs. None of the males in my group had submitted his name to the others for that honor.

The next day when I got to homeroom there were two names on the blackboard for a run-off for the male to be listed as "most popular." One name was that of the class president, the other name was mine! I couldn't believe it! How could it have happened? The class president had lettered in football, and I hadn't even been the waterboy. It must have been some miracle - a gift from God for my being good. And as I voted for myself, I made a pact with God to be even better in the future if He would give me this moment in the sun.

It wasn't to be. I lost by one vote. I was Mr. Almost Most Popular. As I left school that afternoon, the results having been announced, a girl I barely knew came up to me. She wanted me to know she thought I should have gotten "most popular" title, but she hadn't voted for me. She didn't vote for me because she had been told I desperately wanted to be voted "most likely to succeed." Since she liked me, she wanted me to get the superlative I wanted.

Hers was the vote that would have cinched it for me. One more vote for me, one less for the other candidate. For a moment I hated her. How could she have been so stupid as to thing I would want "most likely to succeed" over "most popular"? It was all her fault.

Later at home I came to a semblance of my senses. I was the one who had done me in. I was the idiot who thought a person couldn't be liked unless he was a letterman. I had minimized the value of being friendly, cordial, and helpful and all those other awful adjectives. My class was less myopic than I. They saw the total picture whereby I saw only the limited view. All the time I had been gnashing my teeth over not being a sportsman, they were seeing in me traits they considered to be just as important.

I was voted "most likely to succeed", and maybe my "almost win" of the "most popular" superlative made me succeed a little more in life than I would have otherwise. Never again did I feel myself to be less because I was not a sports addict. I found there truly are different strokes for different folks, and this difference does make the world go `round.

The cheerleader and I didn't last through college. She married someone else, but I don't think he lettered in sports either. I married the prettiest girl in St. Petersburg, Fla., and she is even less athletic than I am. Somehow, we produced two boys who hold their own on various teams. But whether or not they ever letter is not important to me. I just want them to be the best at anything they want to try.

So if you are in high school and you feel like the world's greatest failure because you aren't on the football team, cheer up. There is life after high school. And your life can be the best one possible.

Even now you might be the most popular person in your class and you don't even know it. Quit knocking yourself down. Chances are the people around you see more in you than you do yourself.

As for me, I still like the movies. I still like books. I still would rather watch the Oscars than the Super Bowl. I still hate to sweat, and I still like to rest. But most of all, I now like me. And that is the most important success of all.

Mother Liked those Sad Songs

A few days ago I was driving to work with the car radio blaring, and out came the melodious voice of Kenny Rogers. Kenny was singing about a man who killed his girlfriend because she was unfaithful. Because of this he was hanged and then buried beneath the tree from which he was hanged. The story of this "unknown lover" was carried about by the breeze as a warning for all souls who fall for an untrue woman.

My first thought upon hearing this song was–Mother would have loved it. Now that may seem like a strange statement from a devoted son to make about his mother. But then you never knew my mother. On the one hand Margaret Virginia Kershaw Cooper was as sane, loving, intelligent and compassionate as anyone you would want to know. But on the subject of grief and sadness she was a little off-center. And that made me love her even more.

My aunts and uncles used to tell me about what she was like as a little girl. Mother would get all embarrassed when they would tell these stories, but she never denied them. Her siblings told me she was nicknamed "the buzzard."

A cemetery was located across a field from their house in Gadsden, Alabama. Whenever there was a funeral mother would take off across the field. "There goes 'the buzzard,'" the others would shout. And off she would go to take her place at the edge of the grave site. There she would listen to the minister intone the attributes of the dearly departed. With each word the somber little girl would gasp and sob as the tears rolled down her face. Many in the crowd would wonder about the poor little girl who was so emotionally jolted by the death that had occurred, and many would pat her and whisper words of encouragement as they passed by.

Why my mother was attracted to funerals, I can't say to this day. All she would ever tell me is that she felt drawn to show grief over anyone who died. I accepted that explanation then, and I accept it now. Maybe the psychiatrists who are reading this can give more insight. I know it is eccentric behavior of a modest degree, but I can think of many traits that would have been worse.

This obsession with sadness also spilled over into her love for morbid songs. Any song that told a story about lost love, unrequited love, or unspoken love was a favorite to her instantly. To this day I can remember being rocked to sleep by her and listening to her sing about a man who got mad at his girlfriend and "beat her and banged her and slung her around. He threw her in the river where he knew she would drown." If I wasn't asleep by the time, she finished it, I would beg her to sing it again.

Now don't think I am an advocate of violence against women. And most certainly my mother was not. It was just that she loved the passion and power of the storied songs and passed that love on to me. The more convoluted the plot of the story, the more I enjoy the song.

The obsession with funerals was not passed on to me. I hate them, hate everything about them. But the sad songs, sad books, and sad movies are something I care about just like she did. Most of the time I have to listen to country music to get a real sad story in a song. Pop music, especially rock, does not lend itself to this specialty. Though I do have to say, Harry Chapin was the master when it came to writing and singing songs that were full-fledged stories. "Taxi" and "WOLD" are classics of this type.

I do seek out sad movies whenever I get the chance. However, I feel today's movies aren't cut from the same cloth as the tear jerkers of the 40s and 50s. Some thought "Terms of Endearment" was a teary film. For me it was only a minor clog of the throat. When you have been through such Kleenex killers as "Imitation of Life," "All Mine to Give," "Old Yeller" and "Brian's Song," then "Terms of Endearment" isn't even worth serious thought. Those movies I named went straight to the heart and pounded it with pathos.

I had only been married a few months when "Brian's Song" came on television. My poor bride thought she had married the wimp of the western world as she saw me dissolved by the content of this epic. She got a little teary, but I was wiped out by the story, especially the music. And the bad thing was that the sadder it got, the more I loved it. My mother lives on now through me.

So now I have a new song to listen for on the radio–Kenny Rogers and his ballad about the "unknown lover." And maybe Kenny picks those songs to sing because his mother loves them too.

Thinner Isn't a Curse

One of the best-selling novels of last year was a book by Richard Bachman called Thinner. The book was really written by Stephen King and Richard Bachman is a fictitious name, but that's another column. Anyway, in Thinner a bright but overweight attorney is cursed by a gypsy. The curse is one word – "thinner." From that point on the overweight lawyer begins to lose weight. Does that sound like a curse to you? It sounds like a blessing to me.

Being overweight is no fun, unless you count the fun of eating the food which makes you overweight. I love to eat. I love to think about eating. I plan meals in my mind. Once a week I make a sacred pilgrimage to a place in Macon where it is all you can eat for $3.75. Those folks don't make money off of me. It is strictly pig-out time.

There is another restaurant I frequent in Macon. I was there recently. For some reason the people behind the counter started talking to me about my tie. It is a perfectly normal tie, blue with some green blobs on it. The blobs are in the pattern of the tie and are not leftover food. But the remarks concerned the fact that the second end of the tie was almost up to my neck.

Patiently I explained that if I made the two ends equal the tie would stop midway down my stomach. I also explained this was a problem with most ties, and it was the manufacturer's fault and not my own. I thought I explained it all satisfactorily until one of the guys behind the counter said he had the same trouble, and I quote him – "I don't have a big stomach or a fat neck."

This is the same group that tried to tell me how much they missed me a few weeks ago. I had not been eating at this place as I had been trying a soup diet for the winter.

"Where have you been?" asked Connie the counter girl as I walked up to place my order.

"I have been eating at the soup bar," I explained. " I have been on a soup diet."

"Didn't work," the entire group chorused.

Honestly, I felt I was living my life at "Cheers" and they had cast me as Norman.

California Dreamin' and Happiness

What is it about California that fascinates us? The warmth of the state as well as just the name itself seems to be a basis for dreams, hopes and aspirations. At least it always has to me. From my earliest memories on I have dreamed about California and what life out there would be like.

Not only did I dream about living in California, I used the term California as my personal dream of happiness and fulfillment. Whenever things would be going bad in my life I would think just wait until I get to California. Then I could put aside the hurts or horrors of the real world and retreat in my mind to that Utopian place where all dreams came true and all hopes were fulfilled.

Not only did I fill myself with this "dream of California," I also infected my cousin Lyllis with this same dream connotation of the word. She too would put aside her hopes and frustrations with a "just wait until we get to California."

You should have known Lyllis--she was a one in a million girl. She was not what you would call traditionally pretty, but there was an oddness about her that made people look twice. Of course, she was also a kook, and that helped attract attention too.

In Clinton, S.C., Lyllis was really a thorn among roses. She was the first girl I knew who smoked, drank or ran around. By running around I don't mean she was promiscuous, but she did run around. I was her confidant, and she told me everything. And believe me she had a lot more to tell than I did.

She also had a Hollywood fixation. Well, we both did. She was Liz Taylor, and I was James Dean. Lyllis took it a lot more seriously than I did. She was into the Cleopatra makeup look; I just wore a red jacket like James Dean. When he was killed in a car wreck, that kind of ended my identification with him. But not Lyllis. She never forgave him for getting killed and was mad at me for weeks because I wouldn't go into mourning with her.

She always knew when we got to California we would meet Liz Taylor, and she would adopt us both. I could never see Liz Taylor as a mother figure, but Lyllis could and did. She read somewhere Liz liked black clothes, and for the longest time she wore only black skirts and sweaters with silver lip gloss and the heavy makeup around the eyes.

After high school I went off to college. Lyllis stayed at home and planned for our eventual move to California. Then I messed things up by deciding to go to law school. Lyllis moved to Columbia, S.C., where law school was and worked while I studied. She still had hopes of the migration west.

It wasn't that I didn't still dream about California; I did. But reality was butting in on my dreams. I had to think about how I was going to make a living, and also I wanted to meet someone and fall in love and settle down. Then I would go to California.

By the time I got out of law school it was time for me and Uncle Sam to have a talk. He talked, I listened, and joined the Air Force. This was the last straw with Lyllis. She packed her bags and joined her family in Kentucky where they had moved during my college years. She said she would save her money and find California on her own.

While I was in the service, we kept in touch. I would still write to her and tell her how much I needed "California" and how I felt like I would never find it. The dream was still in me, but my destiny was on hold for four years in the service.

Before I ended my career with the Air Force, I found the woman I wanted to marry, and marry her I did. Reality hit home with a thud then as I worried about supporting two. California was once more put on hold as I found the right job to give us a decent living. Still in my more somber moments I would write to Lyllis and say, "Some day, California." But I meant the journey would be for three of us, and I don't think Lyllis ever liked sharing the dream.

On July 10, 1972, I wrote my last letter to Lyllis. I told her about taking my wife to the hospital and about my nervousness while I waited for our baby to be born. I closed the letter by telling her how it felt to hold a part of yourself in your arms. And I told her that when I looked into his eyes I saw California.

I haven't heard from Lyllis in years. Maybe she made it to California on her own. Somehow I doubt it. I think she is the type of person who always keeps her dreams in the future and never puts feet to her plans. But I hope she did find a type of happiness.

Who knows! Someday she might just drive up to where I live in Perry and tell me she wants to see California. He has gotten pretty big now, and we call him JJ for Jackie Jr. Somehow California just didn't seem an appropriate name to weigh a kid down with. But just as I told Lyllis in that July 10 letter, he is California to me—and always will be.

He's My Friend and I like Him

Friends are special people who get you through the bad times and share your good times. They come in all shapes and sizes, all ages and personalities.

Let me tell you about my friend Chuck. He is one in a million, at least in my book. We have been friends since the beginning of time. I can't remember when he wasn't around to talk to, laugh with, share with. If you have one friendship like Chuck's in your life, you are ahead of the game.

Back when we were growing up Chuck was smarter than me and more athletic than me. It wasn't hard to be more athletic, but I was pretty smart. But Chuck was smarter and in his subtle way he never let me forget it. He also considered himself more realistic and was constantly telling me I lived in a dream or fantasy world. Maybe I did.

Chuck and I went through grammar school, high school and college together. After college Chuck got married -for the first time. He married a girl who had just finished her freshman year in college but was eager to be wed and start a family. Chuck and Sally were a blissfully happy couple as they stood at the front of the church and were wed. I was right there serving as an usher for my friend Chuck. How I envied him. He now had everything I wanted. I was going through a bad time as the cheerleader I had been dating for ninety-nine years had broken up with me. I was convinced the right girl had passed me by, and I was settling in to a long bout of self-pity.

Chuck and Sally were determined to find "Miss Right" for me. While I was in law school I would go to see them and see the joys of married life. They tried fixing me up with one girl after another, but nothing ever came of these romantic arrangements. Chuck thought he could do everything, but he was a complete bust as a matchmaker for me. He refused to take the blame but said I was still living in that fantasy world and still seeking the "perfect" woman.

Chuck's advice to me was to marry a younger girl and raise her up like I wanted her to be. That was what he was doing with Sally. He was sending her back to school and was indoctrinating her with the Chuck way of living. He wanted a woman who could think for herself but would always agree with him. Well, he got that with Sally, or at least part of it. After two children and a college degree Sally thought for herself and decided she could do without Chuck.

In truth Chuck was not too broken up over this breakup as wife No.2 was waiting in the wings. That was another part of Chuck's philosophy — never let yourself get too attached to one woman. Fine advice for me. I was still looking for one woman.

Wife No.2 was Susie. She had been married at an early age and had two children. She didn't have a college degree. I only met Susie once and that was when she and Chuck were on their honeymoon. They dropped by to see old lonesome me and spent a few hours. Susie looked like a sweet enough girl. She sat there doing needlepoint while Chuck and I chewed the fat. Marriage No.2 looked like a winner.

While No.2 marriage progressed, I met "Miss Right." Chuck said it would never last. My bride was too assertive, too independent, too pretty. I would never be able to raise her up to be what I wanted. That's what Chuck said. My friend Chuck, already with wife No.2.

One day I got a call from Chuck, and he said he had decided to send Susie back to college to get her degree. Warning bells went off in my head, but I kept my mouth shut. Chuck was never any good about accepting advice, especially from me. He was the counselor in our friendship, I was the listener. So I didn't express my views of gloom and doom about this idea. Besides Chuck wanted a wife who could think for herself but who would also agree with him. He got the first part again. Susie got her degree, and she also got herself a divorce from Chuck.

This time Chuck was distraught. I got late night phone calls from him, and he would moan, groan and tell me it was all over. Since Chuck and I are the same age — except he is 12 days older — I didn't like hearing life was over. But that was Chuck. He had dropped from the heights to the pits. He began to write morbid poetry about souls in torment through loss of love. I would listen to this type of depressive verse and then try to get back to sleep. Believe me it wasn't easy. His poetry was like Rod McKuen with a terminal disease.

Suddenly Chuck the philosopher gave way to Chuck the playboy. Now his calls were about the dating life and the singles scene. Masters and Johnson could have studied him. Once again I listened to all of this and then tried to get back to sleep. It wasn't easy then either. But then it became obvious that there is nothing sadder than a 40-year-old man trying to act 25. A swinging single he was not meant to be. It took a few months of raving about the good life before he came clean and told me how much he hated it all. He was tired about asking about signs and zodiacs. He was tired of worrying about gaining weight and losing hair. He was tired of playing the field when he had to carry the ball all the time. He wanted to be married again, but this time out he couldn't find "Miss Right."

This story has a happy ending. Chuck got married again. Wife No.3 is older than either of the previous two were at the time they wed Chuck. She has a degree and a master's. She and Chuck seem to be doing fine. The secret this time out, well Chuck says the secret of a happy marriage is to find someone who really likes you. He claims neither of the first two ever really liked him. If they had, they would have tried to change him rather than just biding their time and then hitting the divorce court.

As for my marriage, after 16 years he thinks it might work out after all. But he keeps giving me advice on how to make it last, advice I rarely use. But I let him keep on talking. That has always been the way with our friendship. He talks — I listen. He's the realist — I am the dreamer. He knows it all — I know a little.

Friendships are funny. They take different shapes and sizes, different roles and aspects. Mine with Chuck is one in a million. I don't want to be like him. I don't want my sons to be like Uncle Chuck. But he's my friend, and I like him. And when he needs me I will be there for him just as he has always been there for me. And like the song says, that's what friends are for.

Norine Was One Really Nice Lady

We have lived in Perry, Georgia, for almost fourteen years now. There was a period of two years when we forsook the hospitality of Georgia for the glitter of California, but we knew Georgia was more of a family place so we headed back. Back to Perry and back to the town we loved.

The first time we ever drove through Perry I noticed a house located right downtown. It seemed to be a part of the charm of the quiet town—a house in the old style tradition that was firmly fixed in the center of the commercial district. Later, I found that this was Norine's house and that the lady who lived there was the essence of everything good in Perry.

Norine's house was located close to the bank, the church, and the doctor's office, and was within walking distance of the post office. This enabled Norine Jones easy access to all the areas she needed to visit during her day. Her stepdaughter worked at the bank, she played the piano at the church, her doctor took care of her health needs, and the post office was where she mailed out her correspondence.

Norine Jones was a town legend in Perry even before we arrived. At that time she was in her seventies and knew everything about Perry you would ever want to know. We wanted to know everything and in those evenings that she baby-sat for our two boys, we would return home from a movie and sit and talk with Norine on into the night. She was the most alive person I have ever met, alive in body and mind.

We had worried when we first met her and asked her to baby-sit for us that she might be too old. Boy, were we wrong about that! Norine was younger in mind than either my wife or me. And agile too. We would come home and find her crawling around on the floor with our baby boy. He loved his "Norine, Norine, the beauty queen" and we did too.

As soon as we met Norine her house took on a great importance to us. Whenever there was a parade in Perry we watched it from the front porch at Norine's house. From that vantage point my boys could get a clear view of Santa Claus and any other celebrity who happened into town.

It was also to Norine's house I ran that night that Terry told me it was time to get to the hospital for the birth of our second son. Out of my car and across her lawn to Norine's house where our son JJ would stay until my folks could get to Perry to keep him. How excited he was about the chance to sleep at Norine's house, and how safe I felt leaving him there.

Norine became a part of our family. The great-grandmother that every child should have, or the wonderful great-aunt that every adult should have to confide in or share dreams with. We didn't take this part of our family to California with us, but we did keep in constant touch. She always wanted to know when we were going to come home. And when we finally did drive back to Perry there was Norine's house still standing strong to welcome us back.

There were times when we thought Norine might lose her house. The city wanted the land for a parking lot or some other modern concept. But each time they couldn't stand to upset this lady the whole town loved so well. So Norine's house remained.

Earlier this year Norine Jones died. She would have been ninety on her birthday. I grieved for her and I missed her. But her memories are alive and well in my family. Still I hated to think that how generations of families living in Perry would never know about this wonderful woman. I thought how her house would be torn down, and the progress of Perry would erase the beauty of this structure—Norine's house.

A few weeks ago I learned a local businessman had bought Norine's house. And wonder of wonders, he wasn't going to tear it down but was going to enhance the structure and make it a Victorian restaurant or something of that nature. The renovation has already started and Norine's house hasn't looked so good in years.

A few days ago I happened to be standing in front of Norine's house when some tourists or new people to Perry were walking by. They had a small boy with them who was asking about the house and who lived there. His parents didn't know, so I took the time to tell them about Norine's house and about Norine herself. The little boy said she sounded like a really nice lady, this "Norine, Norine, the beauty queen." How right he was. How very right he was.

Having a Wedding Without Stress-induced Sweat

This has certainly been the summer of weddings. From Caroline to Fergie, marriage fever has been in the air. A few weeks ago a friend of mine got married, and in the spirit of the occasion I agreed to sing two songs at the wedding. There were two miracles involved in this situation. One was that he asked ME to SING, and the second was that I did. As a rule I don't do windows and I don't do weddings.

The first song I sang was "The Rose," which was initially made famous by Bette Midler. The second was "A Long and Lasting Love," made popular by Crystal Gayle. Neither of those ladies has anything to fear from me. I have not taken over their songs except for that one special hour at the Methodist Church in MacRae.

When I sang there wasn't a dry eye in the house, mine included. I don't know if it was the pain to the ears or the sweetness of the occasion. I hope it was the latter. An organ playing and two people very much in love can change the ordinary to the blessed. This is what happened to me and those two songs. The love of the couple made the music even sweeter.

While I watched the ceremony of these two friends, my mind raced back to my own wedding in June 1970. That too was a hot summer month, and our wedding was in St. Petersbury, Florida. Even though we were getting married at eight o'clock at night, it was still hot. It is always hot in St. Pete. And when I get hot I sweat. Not perspire but good old "like a pig" sweat. On the night of the wedding ceremony I was hot and nervous.

My bride to be did not see me on the day of our wedding. We followed all the old traditions. So until we were at the altar that night she had not seen my sweaty face, or my almost sweaty face. Prior to the ceremony my sister-in-law, the nurse, came to where I was dressing. With an hour to go to the ceremony the rivers of water were already flowing from my brow.

"You look like you fell in a river," she said.

"I know," I responded.

"We have to do something about that," she said.

"I know," I responded.

"Do you trust me to fix it?" she asked.

"I do," I responded, rehearsing my vows.

So my sister-in-law, the nurse, sprayed my face with antiperspirant. She covered the entire balding mass except for my eyes, where she had affixed cotton gauze. And sure enough the sweat stopped. I looked into the mirror and saw a dry face staring back at me.

"You're wonderful," I cried.

"I know," she responded.

Now it was time for me to go to the church. As I started out the door, I noticed my face was beginning to feel a little tight. By the time I got to the church I felt like a prune. My lips looked like Clara Bow's. But my face was still dry EXCEPT for my eyes.

Around the eyes my body had found the outlet for the perspiration—excuse me, sweat—which was backed up inside my face. Moisture poured from my eyelids and from the patches of unsprayed skin beneath my eyes. On the happiest occasion of my life I looked like a weeping willow.

So if you ever want to see the pictures of my wedding be prepared for a shock. My bride is looking at me with curiosity and love. She appears more than a little apprehensive. And well she should be. I look like a ghoul. More correctly, I look like "Rocky Raccoon," two dark eyes on a sea of white.

There is a lesson here. If God had wanted your body to stay dry, he would have put antiperspirant in your bloodstream. Take it from the "Raccoon man," I know.

Legends about My Relatives

When I was a little boy growing up in South Carolina one of my favorite pastimes was listening to my parents talk about what it was like when they were growing up. Both my parents came from large families. Mother had eight brothers and sisters. Daddy had seven. Mother grew up in Gadsden, Alabama, and Daddy in Clinton, S.C.

In Daddy's family there was always a problem of finding a place for all the kids to sleep. My grandparents ran a boarding house, so when a boarder needed a room and there wasn't one available, the kids doubled or tripled up.

My two aunts, Alma Ruth and Lillian, always shared a room. They had been close from childhood, since there was only a few years' age difference between them. And they were the only girls in a family full of boys. Daddy said they used to talk from sunup to sundown—in fact they carried it on over into their sleep.

Now, the legend in the Cooper family is that Aunt Alma Ruth and Aunt Lillian shared their dreams. I don't mean they shared them in conversation during the daylight hours; they shared them in their sleep and would converse with one another about what was going on. Now I have never heard about anyone having this happen in their family since this time, and I don't know if it was really true, but my Daddy says it was, so I guess it was.

He said one time he heard them talking and went into their room. Both were sound asleep with their eyes closed. They were talking like they were sitting on the front porch watching people ride by on bikes or in buggies. They talked about who came by and even shared conversation about what they were wearing. Obviously they were viewing the same scene in their heads.

Now I know that sounds weird, but as Ripley said—believe it or not.

The other favorite story of mine about my Daddy's family also concerns actions in the sleep of one of its members. This member of the family was my father. He had a problem with sleepwalking. He also had a horror of buzzards and gypsies. He feared buzzards because when he would go to the well in the back of the Cooper property to draw water, a flock of buzzards would always chase him down the hill.

The reason he feared gypsies is that one of his older brothers told him that gypsies would kidnap kids and sell them into slavery forever. A band of gypsies had been through the community and they were riding motorcycles. These new speedy inventions were supposedly the way they would get the kids out of town before anyone could stop them.

So during my father's childhood he developed the fear of buzzards and gypsies. One night he had a terrible dream that both gypsies and buzzards were after him. He said he ran and he ran trying to get away from them. The problem was that he was sleeprunning. A dog jumped up on him and woke him up - miles from the family home and in the heart of downtown Clinton. To top it off, he was dressed only in his BVD's. This reality was more a nightmare than his dream. He said he made it back to his home and bed in record time.

For months after that my father slept in his pants, but he never made a midnight run back downtown. He did say he heard my aunts talking in their sleep to each other soon after his incident.

"Do you see Tom running?" asked Aunt Lillian.

"Sure do," said Aunt Alma Ruth."He has a bunch of gypsies and buzzards right behind him."

"Run, Tom," they chorused.

Now can any story about your family top that one!

My Friend Hollis Peaked Young

When I sit down to write, it seems my mind always goes back to my childhood in Clinton, South Carolina. In retrospect so much of it seems like a Walt Disney movie. I know it wasn't a perfect childhood, but it surely did come close.

Two reasons I enjoyed my first eighteen years of life were because of my two best friends Chuck and Hollis. Now I have already told you about Chuck in a previous story, but I have not yet told you about Hollis.

Chuck and I were good buddies. We shared everything and were pretty much on an equal basis. Not so with Hollis. I worshiped him. He was everything I thought I wanted to be and wasn't. He was witty, curly haired, charming and a basketball STAR.

From our freshman year in high school on, Hollis was king of the basketball court.

My friendship with Hollis was a subservient one. I picked him up for school every day—in my car. I drove him home after practice each afternoon. I went to his house on weekends to see what he wanted to do. Sometime he would honor me with his presence and sometime he wouldn't. On some nights he just wanted to lie on his bed and listen to the University of Kentucky basketball team play.

Hollis had a girl he liked, but for some reason he picked out the only girl in the school who didn't like him. Of course he didn't really give her a chance to show whether she liked him or not. I don't think he ever asked her for more than a couple of dates. The rest of the time he just loved to talk about and dream about Lori.

A lot of the time he would accompany me and the cheerleader to a movie or to get something to eat. The cheerleader loved having him along. I didn't love the cheerleader loving having him along. I was jealous of her with him and him with her.

During our senior year Hollis was at the top of his form on the court. He made shots he never dreamed of making before and would never make again. He was the captain of the team and as handsome and athletic as he would ever be in his life. It was the golden age of Hollis Arthur.

It is a lot different playing on a local high school basketball team than playing for a college team. And when you are only 5'9" tall you aren't a giant on the basketball court. I went with Hollis when he tried out for a basketball scholarship at Erskine College. He didn't get it. The coach was nice and told him to come out for the team and maybe something could be worked out later. But Hollis never even tried again.

Hollis had been to the top of the mountain, and he had tasted glory. He just couldn't stand the thought of being a mere mortal again like the rest of us. Sitting on the bench would have killed him. So basketball became a thing of the past. And college became a world to be endured. Whenever Hollis and I would get together, all he wanted to talk about was how great high school was.

Hollis graduated from college and became a high school teacher. We still see each other from time to time, but it just isn't the same. His wit has become a little cynical, his curly hair has long ago fallen out, and he races down the basket-ball court only in his dreams. In the past twenty years I have seen him truly happy only a handful of times, and that was when we had our high school class reunions.

On those times Hollis is transformed. The years fall away, and he becomes a part of the young Hollis we knew. We all sit around and reminisce about those days of our youth. Those are long gone days that can never be again but were truly the golden age of Hollis Arthur.

License to Drive Means Freedom

At my house these days all I hear is car talk. And I know it is going to get worse. How do I know? Well neither of my boys is yet at the age where he can obtain a driver's license and already the gleam of car fever is in their eyes. Especially in the eyes of the 14-year-old.

In my day—here it comes kids—in my day the only requirement for a car was that it had four wheels and rolled. The more dented and demented the better. At least that was all I wanted in a car. And basically that was what I got.

My first car was a Plymouth. I don't remember what year it was, but it wasn't brand new or a new brand. It had a past, and with it I had a future. A car would free me to ride the roads. To think. To cruise. To date. I was 14 years old, and I had my driver's license. I was in my prime. Can you believe they let 14-year-old kids have a driver's license back in the '50s in South Carolina? But they did, and I had one.

Of course it took me forever to get it. I would tell all the neighborhood kids to wait until I got home, and I would give them a ride. Off my mother and I went to get the "license." Home my mother and I came – without the license. Have you ever faced the abuse that a neighborhood of disappointed teens and sub-teens can give? "Just wait till next week," I promised.

The next week came. Same plot, same ending. I just couldn't pass that stupid written test. It didn't make logical sense to me. All those stupid questions about car lengths and abstract signs. It might as well have been a test in Greek.

The third week the neighborhood didn't see me off. They had better things to do. I sneaked away in shame. The highway patrolman who gave me the test said it was this time or never. I feared he meant what he said. I dredged up every iota of information I could recall about the driving rules and passed with a 70. Not flying colors by any means but still a pass.

A few weeks later I got the first car of my life – the ancient Plymouth. It was a sick color green on bottom and white on top. The glove compartment was held up by a Band-Aid. You had to slug the dash to get the radio to play. And rust was beginning to eat away at the floor. I considered that a form of air conditioning.

For the next four years that car saw me through the good times and the bad. It was a friend indeed for without those wheels life would have been a downer. Many nights when I would be upset about something, I could get in that car and just ride and ride and ride. Somehow the more miles I covered the less difficult my problems seemed.

We sold the car when I went to college. At the school where I went everything was in walking distance. Plus, the old Plymouth had just about given all it could. One day when I was home from college I went by a junk heap and there on the top of a pile was my old car. The sun hit the shattered windshield, and for a single moment it was transfixed by the glow. Instead of a wreck on top of a junk heap it was a beacon recalling my high school days.

I have never had a car I loved more than that first one. Probably I never will. And I haven't forgotten the excitement of having it be all mine. I envy my sons that experience, but being there to share the moment will help make the debt worthwhile.

That Goodbye Was His Last

They were as close as a brother and sister could be, even though there was an 11-year age difference between them. Plus, there was an intervening brother and two intervening sisters. But in a family of eight children you never know which two are going to be close. You only pray that some of them will be.

In the Kershaw family it was Robert and Virginia. She was the youngest girl, and he was the third eldest son. On the surface it would appear they had nothing in common. But they did. They adored each other. From the time she was a toddler she was his shadow, and he basked in her adoration and love. Even into his teen years he did not forget the little sister who loved him so and would take her to movies and ball games and any other entertainment event she wanted. All of his girl friends knew there was a special woman in his life, and they took care to charm her if they wanted to charm Robert.

Only once did Robert do anything to hurt Virginia, and that happened when she was five and he was 16. A new school year had begun, and Robert, caught up in the excitement of the day, rushed out without telling Virginia goodbye. When she discovered he was gone, Virginia burst into tears, and no one could console her. She finally made herself physically sick and was put to bed.

When Robert got home from school, he learned what his failure to say goodbye had done to her. He rushed to her room and begged her forgiveness. He promised from that day on he would never leave without telling her goodbye. And he didn't.

A couple of years later when Robert was 18 and Virginia was seven, he left one night to go out on a date. As was his custom he kissed her goodbye and told her when he would return.

Virginia had a cold and went to bed early that night. Around 10 or so she woke up and saw Robert standing at the foot of her bed. When she asked what he was doing there he told her he had come to tell her goodbye. Virginia didn't understand, but still she felt a warm glow as he came over and kissed her on her cheek. Then he was gone. And Virginia went back to sleep.

Later that night she was awakened by a commotion in her house. Sadly she learned that her beloved Robert had been killed in a car wreck. He had died a little after 10 that night.

My mother, Virginia, always swore that story was true. Others in her family said she dreamed it. But I like to think it was true. I feel God in his wisdom knew how heartbroken a little girl would be over the death of her older brother and decided to temper that hurt by letting him give her one last goodbye.

Humor Can Help Ease Tense Situation

For the past few months I have read nothing but bad, bad things about the Highway Patrol. You would think that each and every one of those guys in the cars with the revolving lights on top are for sale to the highest bidder. Well I know that isn't so, and down deep you do too. So it is time to get our perspective back about the lone highway patrolmen who are out there keeping our highways safe. And it is also time to get back our sense of humor about them too.

The funniest highway patrol story I know is a true one. And at the time it happened it wasn't funny at all. It happened to me and my family a few years ago. Right around Halloween my wife and two sons were involved in a car wreck. That definitely isn't funny, but it does play a part in this story.

As a result of that wreck, we were given a rental car to drive by the insurance company of the person who plowed into my wife's car. It was a big car, heavy and bulky. Not like the smaller economy cars I was used to driving. So when it came time to pay a visit to my folks in South Carolina, I opted to drive our remaining, intact small car.

"No way," said my wife. "We have every right to drive that big car, and we are going to drive it!"

Never underestimate the determination of a woman who has had her car smashed and her children jeopardized. Driving that big car to South Carolina was only a small price the insurance and crasher would pay. So off to Carolina we went in this tank, me at the wheel, my wife at my side, and the boys in the back.

This side of Milledgeville as we went down a hill, I noticed those wonderful blue lights shining in my rear view mirror. I knew this was not the "K-Mart Blue Light Special," and I was right. It was Mr. Highway Patrol, a strapping youngster of 22 or 23 who immediately became "sir" to me. Highway patrolmen are always "sir" to me. I have never been one to believe in the positive method, I choose the humble instead. Humble and contrite – that's my motto.

This gentleman was most pleasant as he took my driver's license and checked it out. He then stepped into his car to call in the make and tag number of the car. When he got out, I noticed he had taken the strap off the top of his gun holster so he could get to it quicker.

A few minutes later I went up to where my wife and boys were in the "tank" car. "I have some good news and some bad news," I said to them. "The good news is that I only got a warning for speeding. The bad news is that this car is stolen."

You could have heard my children wailing in Canada. "Daddy's going to jail!" they screamed. I almost joined in with them because the patrolman had told me to follow him to the patrol office in Milledgeville, where I would have to stay until this matter was cleared up. It took hours or at least it seemed like hours. I showed them my credit cards, my AAA card, my press card, a picture of my cat –anything to prove I was not the car thief type. I think they believed me, but what good did that do? I was still the driver of a hot car.

Finally the truth came out. I was an innocent victim of the system. The car had been reported stolen. That much was true. It was reported stolen because whoever had rented it before I got it had not returned it on time. When the car wasn't back on the appointed date as stated by the contract, the owner of the car rental place reported it stolen. A few days later the renter brought the car back, but nobody remembered to cancel the complaint to the police. So when the insurance company got the car for me, it was still "stolen" according to the police records.

When it was all over, we all laughed about it. I did, my wife did, the Highway Patrol did. My boys didn't. They were not yet at the age where they could accept the humor in this type of situation. Now when I tell them about it, they laugh but not then. The point is no one was hurt. I guess I could have huffed and puffed at my "false" arrest, but what would that have proved. And I guess the Highway Patrol could have really strong armed me when they found me in the "stolen" car, but they gave me the benefit of the doubt and acted like they believed my story. I wasn't locked up, just kept available until the matter could be cleared up.

They acted like nice, concerned people who really didn't believe I was a car thief. They treated me with caution but with care too. And when it was over I think they were glad I laughed.

I have been stopped since then, and believe me I haven't always laughed. Sometimes I have felt like crying. That is when the politeness and the "sir's" haven't worked. But I have always been treated fairly by the Highway Patrol, and I respect them sincerely for that.

A Former Smoker Confesses - He Loved Every Puff

Yes, it is true, I once was a two-pack a day smoker. It was a dirty, disgusting habit, and I loved it. I was not one of those people who smoked from habit. I was one of those people who loved the taste of tobacco. And I still do. If they would come out and say it is not harmful to your health I would have a pack in my pocket before you could say, "Surgeon General."

When I was growing up in South Carolina in the lazy carefree days of the '50s, drugs and heavy drinking were not things I had to worry about. My crowd was a calm one. We were lovers not fighters, dreamers not drinkers. The only grass we were concerned with was that which grew in our yards and had to be cut, not harvested.

I was not into beer, but a side of my personality did want to be daring. James Dean smoked in "Rebel Without A Cause" and he looked cool, so why wouldn't a cigarette do the same for me. I decided it would, but I didn't want to openly smoke in front of my father. That would be more rebellion than I or he could handle.

So I smoked in my room, and in my car. Somehow my adolescent mind thought if my Dad didn't see it, he also couldn't smell it. My room was a birthplace of smoke that dissipated through open windows into our yard. It is a wonder the fire truck didn't live at our house. Plus the window open trick was fine for the summer, but in the winter it caused me to wrap myself in a blanket as I puffed away.

The strange thing about my fixation with smoking was that at first it made me sick as a dog. I remember clearly lying on my bed, smoking a Kent and watching the room whirl by. Dorothy and her Kansas tornado had nothing on me. When they would call me out to supper my head would be spinning, but my breath would be clean. I spent my allowance on cases of Scope.

When the time came for me to go to college, my Dad still hadn't mentioned my nicotine stained fingers. I was sure I had him fooled. Now I could smoke at college, and he would never have to know. And on the first day of college I bought my first carton of cigarettes. My friend Hollis' mother brought him to Erskine where we both would be going to school. When she got back to Clinton, our home-town, the first thing she commented to her bridge club about was seeing Jackie Cooper standing on a street corner at Erskine with a cigarette in his mouth. She was a tiny woman, but she had a very big mouth.

One weekend toward the end of my freshman year I was visiting at home. I had had a nicotine-free weekend and was in the early stages of withdrawal. My father was driving me back to school, and as I got out of the car he tossed me a pack of Kents and said I might be able to use them. That was all he ever said to me, but it broke the ice.

From that point on I felt free to smoke around him. It also made me feel more grown up. To myself I thought, I must be a man now cause my daddy lets me smoke. Such is the logic of 18-year-olds.

I smoked a total of 18 years. And I enjoyed it all that time. But when my wife became pregnant with our first son, cigarette smoke made her sick so I quit. Then, while I waited for JJ to be born, I smoked pack after pack. Then when she got pregnant with our second son, Sean, I quit for good. He is 11 now so I have been off cigarettes for a total of 12 years.

Do I miss smoking—sure I do. Like I said, I loved the taste of tobacco. Plus smoking is a great social crutch – gives you something to do with your hands. Would I ever start back? Only if God himself gave me a written health guarantee.

Too, I now live with a woman who knows what cigarette smoke smells like. Scope and Certs and all the other mouth fresheners do not throw off her sense of smell. She can hone in on nicotine breath like bees to honey. Lung cancer wouldn't have a chance with me, my wife would kill me first.

Sleeping in a Car Gives Driver a Vote of Confidence

The other afternoon my youngest son and I went to a movie in Macon. As soon as we were on the highway he went to sleep. And he slept until we got to the theater. Now some fathers might be offended by the fact that their son chose to sleep rather than converse. I didn't. That showed me another way he is just like me.

I always had a thing about sleeping in cars too. From earliest childhood on, put me in the car with my father, and I went to sleep. It was the best sleep I had too, an instant deep sleep of complete relaxation. I would get in the car, choose my spot in the back seat, argue over it with my brother, settle down and listen to a few bits of conversation between my parents, and off I would go. No rockabyes needed for me, just the hum of the engine and the vibrations of the wheels.

Hard as it may seem to some of you today to compre-hend, we didn't have a car when I was a baby. I was well up in age before we made that kind of purchase. And we were not one of the poverty level families, we just didn't have a car for pleasure. We had my daddy's bread truck for emergencies and neighbors with cars for everything else.

When I was small, we usually went to my grandparent's house in Gadsden, Alabama, every summer. If my daddy wasn't going with us, we took the train. It was an early morning train called "The Silver Bullet" and it sped us through the night faster than the speed of sound, or at least it seemed that way to me then.

If my daddy was going with us, we borrowed a car. I can remember we always got up early in the morning to start before the sun came up and it got awfully hot. There was a feeling to the world at that time of the morning, and it combined with my sleepiness to all seem unreal. Usually Mother didn't make me put shoes on, and Daddy would carry me to the car so the early morning dew wouldn't wet my feet. I would still be in a state of semi-sleep and might not even remember moving from bed to car when I really woke up. That usually would not be until we reached Columbia, S.C. where we would have our breakfast.

The strongest recollection I have of those car rides is my feeling of complete security. I was enclosed in a car with my daddy at the wheel and nothing and nobody was going to harm me. The family unit was complete and encapsulated in that vehicle. There was no work drawing Daddy away from us and no school or friends to make me wish I was somewhere else.

Today, when we take a trip, I usually do the driving. Sometimes my wife drives, but I never sleep. She is as good a driver as I am and maybe more cautious. But I don't get sleepy and I don't sleep. I don't have any friends whose driving puts me to sleep. I am always wide awake and ready to talk, sightsee, or whatever.

But last summer we went to the mountains with my folks. For some reason we went to their house in Clinton and rode up together. After we had been on the road a while Daddy said he would drive some. I am sure my wife would have preferred me to keep driving as my father is 73 now and tires easily. But it was his car, and he had the right to drive if he wanted to.

I got in the back seat with my wife and kids, and we started off again. We hadn't gone five miles before I fell asleep. I slept until we got to our destination. It was that same deep sleep I had had in the car with him as a child. It was the sleep of absolute security and trust.

So you can see now why I am complimented when my son Sean goes to sleep when I drive. It means he trusts me and is completely secure. I'll do everything I can to keep him that secure at home, on the road, wherever. Just like my daddy did and does for me.

Holidays Just Aren't for Everybody

I don't like holidays. None of them. Halloween, Thanksgiving, 4th of July, Christmas, none of them. Now before you get your dander up let me quickly say, I appreciate the religious significance of Christmas and the patriotic meaning of the 4th of July. I am not against what these days represent. I just don't like holidays.

Over the years it has been brought to my attention that Christmas time affects many people in a negative way. Many, many people get depressed during this time of the year. And supposedly the suicide rate goes up. I don't get suicidal, and I don't get overly depressed. I just tend to want isolation.

From my earliest memory I didn't get excited about the idea of Christmas. I liked toys as much as the next kid, but I didn't want them given to me on Christmas. I wanted them all during the year. When my mother would ask me to make out my list for Santa. I always put down that I wanted a surprise: When she took me to the department store to sit on Santa's knee I always whispered in his ear that I wanted a surprise.

What was the surprise I wanted, who knows? I didn't know then, and I still don't know now. I just know I never got it. And not getting it, I used to make Christmas the pits at our house. We would get up, go into the living room, look at what Santa had left, and then I would go back to bed. It only took a moment for me to see I had not gotten my surprise. I would go back to bed, my mother would cry, my father would be disgusted, and my brother would go on and on about what we had gotten. He had the perfect Christmas gratitude spirit, and it used to make me nauseous.

Eventually I got old enough to act like I had a semblance of good sense. I went through the ritual of opening my presents and oohing and aahing over them, but in her eyes I could see that my mother knew I never got my surprise. I am sure it grieved her to her grave.

Every year that feeling comes back. I long for that great unknown gift that is out there somewhere, but I also know that it will never come true for me. Thankfully my wife and my boys don't ask for the "big surprise" for Christmas. It would kill me to think they wanted something that I could not give to them. Better for me to have this tiny ache than them.

I guess, when I was being created, this lack of holiday spirit was given to me as one of my crosses to bear. But in all honesty, it bothers others much more than it does me. I don't get my surprise, but it really doesn't disappoint me that much as I never expected to get it anyway. I know that is complex, but that is the way it is.

There are a lot of people I have run into during my lifetime who share this lack of holiday fervor. They have been loath to admit it, but it eventually comes out. I have one particular friend who is worse about it than I am. She always calls up a few days before a holiday to ask how I am doing and to report her status to me. We give each other the standard pep talk about how we owe it to our families not to hibernate in our rooms which is what we would both like to do until the holiday is over.

Now that I have confessed all this, I guess you will doubt any wish I ever give for a Merry Christmas. But it is true. I do. I wish for all the true meaning of the season, and also that they get any and every surprise their heart desires. Just because I doubt that my surprise actually exists doesn't mean that theirs won't arrive someday.

Fairy Tales Can Come True

Once upon a time in the magic kingdom of South Carolina there lived a perfectly happy family. There was a father, mother, and two sons. They loved each other and the other inhabitants of their kingdom, and lived a life of idyllic bliss. But even in this magic kingdom the dragon of death could come, and come it did, taking away the beautiful mother and leaving the family sad.

For a while the father just existed, not being happy over anything. But one day he found a new wife and brought her into the family. He was happy, she was happy, the youngest son was devastated. The horrible stepmother had arrived, and he knew from all those other fairy tales just what that meant.

War was declared between the son and his new relative. It was a war of nerves and challenges. The poor father existed in no man's land. He would have ended the war if he had known a way, but the secret key to happiness was not to be found.

Years went by, and the battles became more intense and the sides more hostile to each other. There seemed to be no way to bring the two parties to the negotiating table. Hope for a truce was at a minimum. It was a cold war to be sure.

But while the war was going on the young son grew up and took a bride. And in a few years the young son had a young son of his own. And this young son needed a grandmother.

"Who will be the grandmother for my young son," cried the young man.

"I will," came the answer from the dreaded stepmother.

The whole country was astonished by this answer. Who would have thought the dreaded stepmother would want to be a grandmother to the young son's child. But she did, and in her heart she already was. And when she held the young child in her arms the pain of the long cold war left, and she knew that peace had come to the magical land again.

The stepmother never had to worry about competing with a memory of another grandmother. She was the only paternal grandmother that child would ever know. His father's mother would be a person he would learn about in later years, but she would never take the place of his beloved grandmother.

In the magical kingdom of South Carolina the dreaded stepmother had been replaced by the wonderful grandmother. Strangely enough, they were the same person. They had been all along. But it took a little child to lead his father to that realization.

And they all lived happily ever after.

Reflections from Route 87

Traveling on Route 87 was another happy highway on my journey. I had begun to do more writing, and this took me around the country more than usual. The things I saw as I traveled made me remember more and more about where I had been. As you will read, I continued my love affair with electric fans and ended the year's journey with a miracle at the movies. As Frank Sinatra would say, "It was a very good year."

He's a True Fan of Electric Fans

You've heard the song, "Me and My Shadow." Well my theme song has always been "me and my fan." For all of my life, back into my childhood, I have been involved in a love affair with the electric fan. It is my phobia, my fixation, my fantasy.

It started when my father brought a fan to our home which looked like one engine of a DC-3. This was before air conditioning became common in the American home, so this fantastic fan was a breath of cool air in a house full of South Carolina heat. Such was its strength that it could cool a two-bedroom house on its own if placed in an open window at night so it could suck that cold air in on us.

I loved that fan. I adored that fan. I loved the air it created and the sound it made. It was somewhat like the roar of the ocean, and its rumbling always put me to sleep in a wink. I begged to run it winter and summer, and finally my folks agreed to let it run in the cool season as long as I didn't have it turned right on me.

I remember one warm spring I would rush home from school, turn on the fan and fall asleep. I would wake up for supper, eat, and then head back for my fan. My mother became concerned and took me to the doctor.

"I am concerned," she said, "because he sleeps in front of the fan from afternoon on. He doesn't go out to play. He just lays in front of the fan and sleeps. I am afraid he has some kind of sleeping sickness."

Our family doctor was a man of few words. "Turn off the fan," he said.

She did. I woke up. My fan time was limited to nights. But I had become an addict. I was hooked. On family vacations when we left the fan behind I had trouble falling asleep. I hated leaving home without it. I even took it to college. That caused me some trouble in keeping roommates until I found one who had a weakness for fresh circulating air also.

Slowly I came to realize there is an entire segment of the population who loves motorized air producers. One time when I was in the service, I was sent to Washington, D.C. for training. It was in the dead of winter, snow covered the ground. I had driven up from Georgia, and thus had my fan in the trunk.

Upon being assigned a room I immediately unpacked and placed my fan in a pivotal place. This done I settled down for a nice nap. I had only been asleep a few minutes when a strange sound wakened me.

Sleuthing about I discovered the sound was coming from the adjoining room. I knocked and when the door opened I found I was sharing a bath with a fellow fan of fans. He had brought his with him from Mississippi.

My days of whirring blades were drawing to a close as I found myself falling in love with the Florida girl. We had a lot in common but not our love of fans. It was time to put away one love for the sake of another. The fan went into the closet.

Still life goes on and what goes round comes down. The age of air conditioning settled over America. But then a few years ago fans came back into vogue. You saw them every-where. And when my wife and I built our new house nothing would suit her but to have big ceiling fans in every room. Fans that ran all the time. Put the switch one way and they cool your house in summer. Flip that switch, and they circulate the air and warm your house in winter.

As I type this, my ceiling fan is busily whirring away. Although it is winter, the air it is creating is warm as toast. So I think I will end this as I feel a nap calling to me. And when I dream it might just be about that first love—"Fanny"—when I turned her on she gave me the sweetest sleep I have ever known.

Family's Angel Was There When Most Needed

When I found out my mother had cancer the bottom fell out of my world. I didn't know how any of us would survive the next months or years or however long we had left. I didn't know how I would do without her love, comfort, or understanding, but I knew I would have to. My father wouldn't have time to baby me, and my brother would withdraw into himself as he always did. Things were going to be bad. And they were.

But not as bad as I thought they would be. And that was because of Azalea. That name is pronounced As-a-lee. Where she came from, I don't know. But one day she wasn't there, and the next day she was. And she stayed with us until the cancer had taken my mother.

Azalea was a miracle. I believed it then, and I believe it now. A miracle straight from God. She had to be because she was everything I needed at that time. She was warm and wonderful yet she was firm and strong. I never met anyone like her before, and I doubt I will know anyone like her again.

I think back now, and I wonder when Azalea took care of her own family. She didn't leave our house until nine or so at night, and she was always there at seven in the morning. And this was seven days a week. She had to be there every day because not only was she a nursemaid to me, she was nurse to my mother.

Besides making sure I had clean clothes and had my homework done, Azalea was also there for me when the panic set in. In those moments when my mind would accept the fact that my mother was going to die, Azalea held me and comforted me and told me things were going to be all right. She told me God would get me through it all. I know now He did, but it was His own personal angel Azalea who I looked to as assurance that he would.

I guess I really did think of her as some kind of angel. She came to work dressed in a white uniform, and it was always spotless. As clean at the end of the day as it was at the start. She had to be magic to do the work she did and stay that clean.

A white uniform against her black skin, black skin that some people think we should hate.

I thought about Azalea when I heard a man from Forsyth County say on TV that we should hate all blacks. And that they should never have come over from Africa. If they had never come over from Africa, my mother's last days may have been horrible. They were bad enough, God knows, as it was. But Azalea made them bearable for her and for me.

Hate all the blacks? Never! That would mean hating Azalea, and in a sense that would be like hating God. I loved her then, and I love her now, and I am grateful for her being in my life.

I think there has been an Azalea in everybody's life who has been raised in the magical kingdom of the South. Sometimes we just let hate get in our eyes, and it won't let us see. But I remember, and I think you do too. Don't you?

Important Lessons Learned on Trip

Last week I paid a visit to our nation's capital. It had been years since I was last there, and I wondered how much it had changed. The answer is not much. That's one of the best things about Washington. It doesn't really change. The buildings that are there were built to last, and just as the buildings of Athens and Rome are still around today, so will the buildings of Washington last as long as time does.

But in order to get to Washington I had to put myself on an airplane again. If you know me at all then you know this is not one of my favorite things. I, along with Julie Andrews, like raindrops on roses and whiskers on kittens—not subjecting myself to one of the violations of the laws of physics.

Still, if you have to fly, it is great to be on the airline that is ready when you are. And it is fun to fly first class. I was going on business that involved having all of my expenses paid by someone else. A friend of mine told me I should take the first class ticket they had sent me, cash it in for a passenger ticket and pocket the difference. No way. I am too stingy ever to buy a first class ticket for myself, but if it is being paid for by others, well, I will relax and enjoy it.

Before leaving on this trip, though, I kept having dreams of terrorists attacking the plane. I mean, if I were a terrorist I would attack a plane going to Washington rather than one going to Butte, Montana. So I determined to keep a sharp eye out for any strange looking people.

I was relieved to find everyone on the plane looked OK. That problem solved, I tried to relax during takeoff. The guy in the next seat kept distracting me by waving his hands in the air while the plane was rising into the sky. He also seemed to be chanting something under his breath.

Finally he got through with this procedure and turned and spoke to me. He had a distinct accent, but I couldn't place it. He asked where I was from, and I told him Georgia. He then told me he was from Iran. That cinched it. I just knew I was flying with a terrorist in disguise. Talk about prejudice. He immediately became malevolent and sneaky before my eyes.

I probably would have kept this opinion of him except his next words were how much he loved American movies. With this declaration he changed back into the neat, nice gentlemen he had seemed at first. And for the rest of the flight we talked about the 10 best and 10 worst movies of the year.

Upon reaching Washington I took a cab to my hotel. It was luxurious. I could get used to the kind of treatment they gave me. I could get used to room service. I could get used to hamburgers costing $8. I could get used to someone else paying for everything.

One funny thing did occur when I ordered a hamburger sent up by room service. The lady who answered the call took my order and then asked my name. "Jackie Cooper," I replied.

"You are Jackie Cooper," she said. "Really?"

"Yes I am," I repeated, knowing she had me confused with the other Jackie Cooper who acts and directs movies.

Well that little hamburger came up on a table, set up with flowers, silver service and little mints. The real Jackie Cooper would have been impressed. This Jackie Cooper was impressed. Only the guy who brought it up was disappointed. He had expected the actor who plays "Perry White" in the "Superman" movies. He found a man who is a small tipper from Perry, Georgia.

TV, Teachers Influenced My Life

There was another TV special this week starring Raymond Burr as "Perry Mason." Every time I see that show I wonder if I will ever get a chance to tell Mr. Burr how much he and his alter ego shaped my life.

It all began many years ago in the magic kingdom of South Carolina. I was in the 11th grade at Clinton High School where Miss Shealy, the English teacher, reigned supreme. Now Miss Shealy was one of your lifelong teachers, once she had you in her class she stuck with you for life. She had taught my brother and influenced him enough that he later became an English teacher. Now she was ready for me.

After I had been in her class for a few months, she asked what occupation I had chosen to pursue. I honestly hadn't given it much thought, so I told her I was undecided. She said the time had come when I should decide. She wanted my answer the next day. What Miss Shealy wanted, Miss Shealy got.

That night I didn't give it a second thought. I was too engrossed in the cheerleader I was dating and sitting at her house watching TV. So the next day I was quite unprepared for Miss Shealy when she proceeded to ask me again about my chosen career in front of the entire English class.

Never let it be said that I am not a quick thinker on my feet. I can bob and weave with the best of them. So I reached in the recesses of my mind and pulled out the only vocation that occurred. Good old Perry Mason and the law. I had watched him the night before, and both the cheerleader and I had been impressed with his skills. If the law was good enough for Perry, it was good enough for me.

So lawyer flowed from my lips and into Miss Shealy's brain. "Wonderful!" she chortled. "That is a wonderful career for you." I felt great. Miss Shealy was pleased, and I was of the hook.

Later that week my father ran into Miss Shealy at the grocery, and she told him how pleased she was about my choice of a career. My father the bread salesman was also pleased. He told me so over supper. The pressure was on.

From that day on it was naturally assumed by one and all that I would be going to college AND to law school. I couldn't think of any better alternative so I did just that. Do you know how long law school is? Three years after college! That is one long stretch of school. And all for a career I didn't even like.

But my father liked it. He liked it a lot. "My son the lawyer," he would call me as he introduced me to friends and foes alike. He was the typical Jewish mother trapped inside the body of a gentile male. Once I got my degree, and it turned out to be a J.D. (Doctor of Jurisprudence), I became his son, Dr. Cooper, the lawyer.

Even today when I have left the practice of law behind, he still refers to me in that manner when telling acquaintances about my life. It is never "My son, the writer." The LAW is his dream for me, and reality has nothing to do with it.

Sometimes I think about Miss Shealy and her power over me at that age. She said it was time I decided on a career so I did. No questions asked. Do teachers still have that kind of power over kids? I don't think so.

I also think about the influence TV had on me. If I had watched "Gilligan's Island" that night, I could have grown up to be a castaway. Or if I had watched "Wanted Dead or Alive," I could have become a bounty hunter. Or if I had watched "Ozzie and Harriet," I could have become . . . What did Ozzie Nelson do for a living?

Golden Rule Should Apply at Theaters

I am constantly astounded by the rudeness of people. Of course I probably blunder just as much as they do, but it is easier to see the faults of others than our own. But I do try to avoid doing those things that tick me off completely when others do them.

My current pet peeve is "theater etiquette." It isn't any formal list of dos and don'ts that should be used but rather just common sense. Still for some people who go to plays, concerts, movies, etc., the common sense they do possess is left at home or disappears when they buy their ticket.

Case in point. A few weeks ago my wife and I plus another couple went to the Sandi Patti concert in Macon. It was held at the Coliseum and was by reserved seating. When we got there, an usher took us to our seats, which were already occupied. He asked to see these people's tickets, and they clearly showed the people were in the wrong section.

"You don't understand," the lady in my seat said. "We are all from Hawkinsville and want to sit together."

She seemed to think that answered it all and made no move to change seats. The usher however was insistent that they had to go to their proper seats.

"But we want to sit together," she repeated giving me and my friends a dirty look.

The usher held firm, and the lady and three children got up and moved down to where their friends were sitting. Instead of moving, the adults took the seats and held the children on their laps for the entire concert, which did not make the kids happy. They complained constantly. Which did not make me happy.

Later as the concert progressed there seemed to be a steady processional of people going to the concession stand, to the restrooms, to wherever. It didn't matter what Sandi was singing, these people were going to move. Most of them were teen-age girls who seemed to think the rest of us in the audience were in need of gazing on their beauty. They were wrong. We just wanted them out of our line of sight.

There was an intermission at this show. Why couldn't people wait until then for cokes, souvenirs, and all that? You would think they were on the Sahara dessert rather than at a concert.

As the concert drew to an end, the thoughts of a crowded parking lot began to loom in people's minds. Forget the final song or the encores, these folks just wanted to get back on the road. So the recessional began. Up the aisles with kids and blankets and pillows in tow they came.

I have never asked a performer what this does to the mood of a show. I am sure it affects it. I did go to a Mitzi Gaynor show one time where she stopped her performance to ask a couple coming onto the front row 15 minutes into the show why they were late. The audience applauded her for being bold enough to ask the question.

In the past refreshments were not allowed in most theaters. Not today. Anything goes. Beer and wine can be bought in the lobby and brought into the theater to be consumed during the show. So in addition to talkers and walkers, we now must also contend with drunks.

I guess my question is, why do people go to the theater? For most it is a chance to get out of the house and have a night of entertainment. For others it is a chance to drink, gossip or bother others. Those are the ones I wish would stay at home

The old saying of "Do unto others as you would have them do unto you" is a judge of how you should behave. Think of the things you enjoy the most and how you would not want them ruined. At every play or concert this is how someone in the audience feels. Paying for your ticket does not authorize you to ruin it for everyone else.

One final note. A friend of mine said he went to a revival at an auditorium recently, and people were rushing out to their cars during the closing prayer. For the people determined to be first out of the parking lot, nothing is sacred.

Gimme That Old Time Religion

I am not a person who likes to dwell on the past. I would rather keep my mind on the present and my eye on the future. I think I got this attitude from my father. One of his favorite sayings is "Don't give me the good old days. I lived them, and they weren't that good." I guess everyone who lived through the depression feels that way to some extent.

Still lately I have decided I would like to have back the religion of my youth. That is not a statement my faith has changed. I am talking about the organized religion of my youth. It was the kind that was perfect in my child's eye, and one I could count on to be only full of goodness and charity.

My children today have to live in the world of the media ministers. Whereas I listened to sermons of hellfire and brimstone, they listen to sermons about a God who will kill if not enough money is raised. Believe me I prefer the threat of hell for a life of sin to a threat of death from lack of money. I keep myself from sin as best I can, but I can't give Oral Roberts $8 million.

I was raised Baptist. I am now Methodist. My parents have never recovered from the fact I left the fold. That's the way they are. To them, Baptist is the only religion. I surely didn't leave it out of spite. I just felt more at home with the Methodists.

One thing that confuses me with my "new" religion is the fact that every four or five years the minister moves on to another church. When I was growing up Baptist, we had the same minister for life. The one during my lifetime was Brother Darr. Not Mr. Darr, or Joseph Darr, but Brother Darr, that was his name, his title, his nickname, everything.

Brother Darr was a very formal man. He always wore a suit. I think he slept in his suit. The story was that if you went to his house, he put a suit and tie on before he ever answered the door. I really do think I remember seeing him one day mowing his yard in a suit and tie. I know it sounds silly, but there was something appropriate to me about his always being in a suit. I mean he did represent God, so I thought he should be dressed up.

In those days I never thought about churches having money problems, or ministers wanting raises. There was never an issue about church literature. I was a child. I was protected from those things. It was a great view of religion.

But I guess every generation has its religious problems. Jim Bakker and Jessica Hahn are just today's version of David and Bathsheba. Jimmy Swaggart has the role of Nathan the Prophet. Same play, different cast. Somehow we manage to carry on from age to age. If these players of today are guilty of some sins, as Maude would say, "God will get them."

I long for the old time religion, but I know that my view of it and life are not possible anymore. Children see through a glass darkly while adults have the blinders removed. It's the price we pay for being adults. But wouldn't it be nice to have one place where the pettiness of the world could not intrude.

Sisyphus was the man in legend who pushed rocks up the hill for eternity. Each time he would get his load near the top it would escape from him and roll back down to await him again. That's the way perfection is. We can work on it and work on it, but just when we think we might be getting there, it rolls back down the hill to wait for us to try again.

Family Absence Makes His Heart Grow Fonder

As I write this, I am only days away from my 17th wedding anniversary. Seventeen years! That's impossible! Sometimes I feel like I am only 17 years old. But it is 1987. And I did get married in 1970. So that makes 17 years.

When you have been married 17 years, you do begin to realize that you and your life have changed. Like this week for instance. My wife and two sons went to Florida to visit her parents. No big thing. I could make it alone, on my own. I did it until I was 28 years old, and I did fine.

The first thing I did when they left was go out and buy a big box of cheese tidbits, many cans of tomato juice, and the biggest sack of M&Ms I could find. Adultery never enters my mind. Pigging out does.

Terry had also left me a big bowl of tuna noodle salad to eat for a few days. I ate it all the first day. The whole thing. And loved it! Loved the cheese tidbits and the M&Ms too.

That took care of the first day. But not the first night. As darkness fell this house got bigger and bigger. It was just me and the cat, Fluff. And she was bigger coward than I am. Whoever made up the term "fraidy cat" had Fluff in mind. Every time I went downstairs for something I would pass by her at the bottom of the steps, and she would jump 20 feet and run. A bolting cat can prove to be pretty unnerving.

To try and calm her down, I fed her. Three cans of cat-food later she was still a nervous wreck. A fat nervous wreck but a wreck just the same. And she cried. I had never heard a cat cry like this. She cried and cried and cried. Terrible, tragic mewing sounds. And I could have sworn she was saying, "JJ, JJ, JJ." That is the name of my oldest son and her favorite in the family.

Someone told me once that their cat could talk. I couldn't decide who was crazier, that lady or her cat. Well now I have new respect for her 'cause if my cat can cry and call for JJ, then her cat can probably talk too.

About the time I finally got the cat calmed down my youngest son Sean's radio came on. It has one of those automatic alarms, and it came sneaking on. I could have sworn there was someone in the house with me. It took hours, or so it seemed, before I realized I didn't have a singing burglar in the house.

With all this commotion I decided to retreat in sleep. That has always worked for me before. Whenever I get depressed, I can sleep. This time it didn't work. I was wide awake. I turned on the overhead fan. Fans always put me to sleep. That didn't do it. The house was too quiet. There were creaks and moans in the structure of the house I had never heard before when Terry and the boys were here.

This called for desperate measures. I got the cat upstairs with me and locked off the bottom of the house. I turned the air conditioning way up, got the box fan I used before we got ceiling fans and turned that right on me, and put the electric blanket on the bed and turned it on too. It worked. I slept like a baby.

Terry and the boys will be home the day after tomorrow. They will find a rested husband and father awaiting them. The cat will probably still be a wreck, but I will be fine. Fine until I see what all this electricity use has done to our utility bill.

Seventeen years! How did I ever survive without being married, or without having kids? Before marriage I thought I was living the good life, but believe me—the good life is now. It's funny how even the pain of missing your family can make you feel good.

The Bionic Man Strikes Again

A few days ago I was talking with a friend, and we were discussing aging. The particular topic of conversation was when did we stop looking forward and start looking back. My friend said he thought it was when he got out of college. I disagreed. I thought it was after I got married. But be it college or marriage, there does come a time in our lives when we spend more time looking backward than we do looking ahead.

There also comes a time in our lives when we start being the parent in a sense to our parents. It just happens. No longer are they our buffer against the woes of the world, but we are theirs. And I guess that is as it should be. I know I learned in high school that I could not really go to my father with my problems. He had enough on him, and I would just have to muddle through as best I could. It was our relationship, the way we had worked things out between us, and the way that suited our personalities best.

That isn't to say my father wouldn't help out if I needed him. He would. But he isn't there to make decisions or to offer words of wisdom that I want to take. He is more there as a loving soul who is fun to be around. The perfect grandfather, so to speak.

Lately I am thinking of him as the bionic man. He has had his share of ailments lately, but modern medicine is doing him up just fine. Plus he is one of those rare people who does not feel much pain. He has never had a headache. Never. His threshold level for pain is high. So is my brother's. As a matter of fact, my brother had a ruptured appendix and didn't know it. Just had some discomfort which eventually caused him to go to the doctor.

Similarly, my father went to the doctor a few weeks ago. He was feeling a little off balance. Well, they discovered his carotid artery (the big one to the brain) was almost totally blocked, and his blood pressure was something like 200 over 135. He was a walking stroke and should have had a headache so big it would feel like the weight of the world was on him. Not him, he just felt a little off balance.

But they did schedule him for surgery. Being the good son, I went to Clinton, S.C., for the surgery. I am in the good son role now. My brother and I keep swapping the good son/bad son identity back and forth. He is in his bad son phase since the D-I-V-O-R-C-E, and I am good as gold.

When I got there, my stepmother and I took up our vigil in the waiting room while the doctor did surgery on my father. I had not gotten there before he went into surgery because they had moved up the time after I had gotten on the road. It was not the good son's fault he was not there. Of course, I am such a morbid soul that I took it as an omen that I would never see my father alive again. I even thought about asking if I could go into the operating room just to have a chance to say good-bye. I controlled that impulse, thank goodness. My father survived the operation just fine without my teary farewell.

Anyway, my stepmother said she wanted to prepare me before I met my father's doctor. That kind of gave me a jolt as I didn't know what to expect. It turns out he was in a wheelchair. I had never met a doctor in a wheelchair. And this guy is a surgeon. I thought it was great that he hadn't let his handicap slow him down. If he is good with his hands, I thought, then what possible problem could it be that his legs were inert. I even thought about that old statement concerning when one sense is removed the others become more acute. If his legs were paralyzed then maybe his hands were even more skilled.

Well, something was done right because, as I said, my father sailed through the surgery. Of course, when he first came out, he didn't look too great. He is 73 years of age, and he had had his main artery split open and cleaned. Plus, he didn't have his teeth in, so he couldn't speak plainly. When I went into his room in the Intensive Care Unit where they had put him as a precaution, he mumbled something that sounded like, "I'm in pain."

I almost panicked. I mean my father doesn't ever feel much pain, so he must really be hurting. I leaned over him again to make sure I had heard correctly. "I'm in pain!" is what it sounded like again. Finally I got right over his face and put my ear to his mouth. "I'm so glad you came!" was what I heard.

The next day my father checked out of ICU. The next day after that he checked out of the hospital. The bionic man had struck again. He was back in his own home, and I called to check on him just like a parent with a child. Just like a full circle of love. Just like things should be.

'Roughing It' Means Staying at a Cheap Motel

It is summertime, and summertime means camp to millions of American youth. And as I write this both of my sons are at camp. The 15-year-old has gone to debate camp for two weeks. At least he was 15 when we took him there. In the two phone calls that he allotted to us he sounds more like 25 now. Freedom does wonders for maturity. It is making me an old man with worry.

The 12-year-old is at church camp. It will only last four days. That is more than long enough for me to be without both my children. It is not that I don't love their mother and enjoy her company, but I like the sound of big feet clunking around the house. The poor cat had just gotten used to the boys being home from their vacation in Florida, and now they are gone again. She has taken to her favorite spot under the dining room chair and refuses to discuss the matter with anyone. She is playing the role of abandoned cat to the hilt.

But all of this just brings back memories of my days at camp. When I went as a camper, I hated it. I begged not to be made to go. But somehow my folks thought it would be good for me. I am such a different parent. If either of my boys had said the word, home they would have stayed.

Anyway, off I went to camp for a week. To a land of snakes and other slimy things. Off to a land where they didn't have a movie theater within walking distance. Those were going to be seven lonely days. And they were.

My friend who went with me to camp was a really nice guy, but he couldn't swim. At the camp where we went they used the buddy system. You had to have a buddy with you to swim. Since he couldn't pass the swimming test, I couldn't swim. So we played Ping Pong. Over and over again we played Ping Pong. I could have taken on the entire Chinese nation, I became such an expert. Even through my tears I could slam a point home.

Still, something must have struck me right about camp life because years later I went back to this same camp as a counselor. Yep, volunteered, signed up and off I went. A summer in the fresh air in the cool of the mountains. It was to be a delight. And to some extent it was.

The problem was that I had to cope with homesick campers and bedwetters. For some unknown reason, my cabin always had more mattresses drying out front than any other. Other campers—and counselors—made cruel remarks to me and my boys about our aversion to dryness.

Then too, by this time I had become a smoker. Counselors were not allowed to smoke in the cabins in front of the boys. We had to wait until night time when we went to the lodge after the campers were asleep and in the care of the assistant counselors. Nobody waited till then. We had a path beat into the woods by the second day, to where we could puff away in private. We were breathing pure mountain air, but we were polluting it with cigarette smoke at a rapid rate.

And what about girls. Well, when we first got there, we had a joint party with the girls camp across the lake. We raved and ranted about the dogs who came to the girls' camps as counselors. None of us were going to have anything to do with them. Never! Never ever! That lasted about a month. Then a miracle occurred. Those plain-as-could-be counselors began to be transformed by the mountain mist. They became our dream women. We looked forward to those joint parties.

By the end of the summer I was involved with one of the counselors to a serious extent. I was one step away from breaking up with the cheerleader at home. But luckily camp ended. I made a trip over to see Cathy Counselor the day after I got home and learned the mountain mist had faded. What had seemed beautiful in the Shangri-La mountains became ordinary in the South Carolina sun. A secluded summer in the mountains had almost altered my perspective.

When I think back to my days as a camp counselor, I realize I was never in better shape. I was never as tan and was never so energetic. I was never so starved for female companionship.

Still, that summer I learned, with my campers, to shoot a bow and arrow, hike up a mountain, get up early and see the sun come up, swim in a cold lake, paddle a canoe and cross weave a bracelet. I never did learn how to make a fire from sticks, sleep on the ground, do a flip on a trampoline or touch a snake. There is only so much you can learn in a summer.

I hope my kids are having a great time at camp. Better than I had as a camper. That, to me, was the pits. As a counselor it got better. Still I never did learn to appreciate the wonders of the great outdoors, and to this day my idea of roughing it is to stay at a cheap motel. I have met the enemy, and it is nature. We looked each other over and decided to make a truce. I don't bother it, and it doesn't bother me. Those of you who like to camp can have my spot forever. I give it to you gladly.

He Was Down, Out in Beverly Hills

A few weeks ago I had to go to California on business. If you have to go somewhere on business, California is the place to go. Of course it also meant I had to fly since the bus trips to L.A. take too long. The thought did cross my mind but only for a short time. I decided what the heck and agreed to fly across the country.

The person making my reservations asked if I had a preference for an airline. I said no. If God was going to toss me out of the sky, He was going to have to choose the means to do it. The agent booked me on Delta. Good going, God.

I called Delta to confirm my reservations the day before I left. An answering machine came on and told me the clerks were busy, but they would not cut me off. "Stay on the line," the unattached voice said. "You will not be cut off." The next sound I heard was a dial tone. Delta and I were in trouble.

Surprisingly, my flight out was great. I almost nodded off to sleep at one point, but then I remembered where I was and decided the pilot needed for me to stay awake. I guarded that plane like a zealot.

We arrived in Los Angeles on time and didn't even cut off the engines as we came in over the ocean. What more could you ask. Still I did kiss the ground when we landed — out of gratitude, not for trying to outdo Tammy Faye Bakker.

The sky was brilliantly clear in Los Angeles. There was not even a hint of smog. If they were trying to make postcards that day, it was the perfect weather for it. When I had lived there, the smog was in full power in July. This was October weather but hotter. One day while I was there, I decided to stroll down to Beverly Hills. I had been to Beverly Hills before so I was familiar with the surroundings. Having just finished a business meeting, I was in gray slacks, white shirt, blue blazer and tie. I also had on new shoes.

Getting to Beverly Hills was easy. Finding my way back was not. Somehow I got turned around and ended up on roads I did not know. I walked for an hour. The blazer came off and so did the tie. I asked for directions. That got me even more lost. By this time the sun was searching out every bare pore on my head, and believe me there are a lot of those. The hairs that are there had shriveled in the heat and left my scalp to cook.

On and on I walked. Why didn't he take a cab? you may be asking. I couldn't find one. All I saw were BMWs, Mercedes, even a Rolls Royce or two. But no cabs. And no buses. I walked on.

My feet began to cramp because of my shoes. I was in pain. I was also getting mad, and lost, then mad again. I decided nobody knew me in Beverly Hills, so I took my shoes and socks off. I guess I probably looked down and out in Beverly Hills, but I was more like hot and ticked. Where is Eddie Murphy when you need him?

After approximately two hours, I made my way back to the Four Seasons (name dropper) and climbed to my room. My head was burnt, and my feet were blistered. Literally with big blisters that the hot pavement had caused. And that night there was a party around the pool. I wore my shoes to the party. I didn't wear them home.

So now I am back from my California trip, and my feet are still blistered, and my head is peeling. There is no grosser sight than a man with big flakes of skin coming out of his head. I know because my family has told me.

So if you are going to California, make sure you take along a map. You never know when you might get lost in Beverly Hills, and the sight of a second Georgian strolling down Rodeo Drive with shoes and socks in hand could damage the reputation of our state forever.

Friends Have a Purpose in Life

Years ago when my wife and I were first married we lived In the town of Rocky Mount, N.C.. I was a brand new attorney practicing real estate law for a company in that town. It was a time of being newly married, new on the job, and making new friends. There were several other couples in the town in exactly the same situation.

One of these couples was Roger and Jennie. We met them through the church — the Baptist Church. This was back in the days when we were still Baptists and had not gone over to the Methodist fold. Anyway Roger was the choir director at that church, and Jennie, his wife, was the organist.

For the year that we lived in Rocky Mount, Jennie and Roger were our best friends. We both had our first child during that year, and that cemented our friendship even further. Then we both moved away. I got a new job, and so did Roger.

Through the years we kept in touch sporadically. Maybe a card here and there, every once in a while a letter, and best of all, a phone call when the spirit moved one of us. But it was not a common thing to talk or hear from them or them from us. Life was too busy and so were we.

But a few years ago Roger called and said they were going to vacation in Florida and would like to stop by on their way down there. That was fine with us, and we made plans to have them visit. I was a little worried about whether or not we would still have anything in common. I worried about what we would talk about. I worried they had changed.

Well from the moment they arrived on that first trip several years ago we started talking, and we were still hollering conversation at each other as they drove off to Florida. There was not a moment's silence between the two couples. It was truly like we had never been apart.

Since that time they have come back every year. And each time it is better than the time before. We laugh, talk, eat, and do very little sleeping. We get a chance to see their son growing up in front of our eyes. Each year he is a little taller, a little more mature.

For some reason Roger and Jennie don't age at all. They still look exactly the same as they did when we were all young and fresh in Rocky Mount. Of course they tell us the same thing. That's what friends are for.

We still don't see each other but once a year. Roger and I talk a little during the year, but we never visit each other except for this one trip. Still, we have somehow become more involved in each other's lives. I send them clippings of some articles I write, and Jennie sends me news about the Louisville Opera where she works.

And our friendship has produced a mutual friend for us in Perry. A couple of years ago the Perry Methodist Church was looking for a choir director. I asked Roger for a suggestion since he knew a lot of good people in that field. He sent me the name of a potential director, and even though he was a Baptist I gave his name and resume to the search committee at the church. He was hired, and my friend Roger is due all the thanks for the wonderful music now emanating from the church choir.

I once saw a play called "Same Time, Next Year" where a man and woman carried on an adulterous relationship one weekend a year over a period of many years. I thought it was a good play but a pretty far out idea. Nobody could remain interested in a person romantically or even friendship wise when they only visited one weekend a year. Now I know it can happen. A good, true friendship can sustain itself indefinitely with a yearly visit. At least this one can.

Now I wonder what would happen if we did live in the same town again. Would we be as close as we are now or would we tire of each other and let the friendship fade? I don't know the answer, but I do know that for now I look forward to the freshness of each new year's visit and the excitement the rekindling of that friendship brings.

Roger and Jennie came to see us last weekend. We talked until two in the morning, got a little sleep, and then they were off. It was wonderful. Their son has gotten a little older in looks, but they still look exactly the same. Just like we do. I know because Roger told me so, and Roger never lies. That is why we are such good friends.

Laughing Helps People Cope

Thomas Wolfe was wrong. You can go home again if it is only for short visits. At least that is the way it works for me. Anything over three days and I get antsy. I also get to feeling like a child again, and I have worked too long and invested too many years into being an adult to go back to being a child—for anybody.

For me home is Clinton, S.C.. I lived there for almost 20 years. I hadn't been back for a real visit in almost seven. By real visit I mean a go home, spend the night, go to church type visit. Most of the times my folks come here or we go through Clinton on our way to somewhere else.

But last week I went home with my wife and two children in tow. And as a surprise for me, two of the people I grew up with planned a Sunday dinner/reunion of all the people who lived in and around Holland Street when I was growing up. They all showed up plus their spouses and children. There were no grandchildren yet. We are still a young-to-middle-aged group.

One of my favorite people from my youth was a girl named Nancy. She is and was big, blonde and boisterous. Nothing comes out of her mouth without a laugh or a giggle. She is still a person constantly in a good mood. If you ever heard Frank Sinatra sing about "Nancy With the Laughing Face," well the song could have been written about her.

She is not the least self conscious about being big. She is not a fat person, just a big woman. I was talking to her about how good she looks, and we somehow got on the subject of weddings and brides.

"I ate myself silly the month before my wedding," she said with a laugh. "It was wonderful to eat anything and everything I wanted."

"Why in the world would you want to gain weight before your wedding?" I asked. "I thought all brides wanted to be their slimmest and trimmest best on their wedding day."

"Jackie" she said, "didn't you ever see those pictures of brides in the homes of women who had gained weight through the years. You couldn't even recognize them as the same person. I knew people like that. And I swore that was never going to happen to me. Nobody was going to come into my home, take a look at my bridal picture and say 'Is that really you!'"

By this time I was rolling on the floor, but Nancy kept going. "I think I have even lost a few pounds since then, and people are always so admiring of a woman who has lost weight rather than gained it. Every girl should pig out before the ceremony and improve later on. It makes everybody happier."

Now you have to admit that has a certain perverse sense of logic. And only my friend Nancy would have been smart enough to think of it. Smart and realistic as well as unique. Nancy was always a person who did what she wanted rather than what people thought she should do. Now I don't mean she defied moral traditions or anything like that. She just did what she thought was right as long as no one else was hurt.

Take the name of her first born son. It Is John Wayne. Nancy married a man named Wayne. When their son was born, she wanted him named for his father, and she also liked the name John. So John Wayne he became. She says the name has been great for him, and he loves it. From pictures he looked to be six feet or more and pretty rugged. I am sure the "Duke" would be proud to have him carrying on the name.

There are gobs of Nancy stories both past and present I could tell you, but that would take up too many pages. So here is one last one. Nancy said they had had "stone soup" for supper the night before. I had no idea what the term "stone soup" meant, but my wife did since she teaches kindergarten, and the term is from a children's story.

Nancy's "stone soup" got its name in this way. She had bought some packets of food, the kind you heat in a microwave or boiling water. Just as she was getting started she had a visitor so she told her daughter to wait until the water boiled and then put the packets in to heat.

When the visitor left Nancy went back into the kitchen to see about the supper. There was a soupy looking mess cooking on the stove. Her daughter had added the packets all right. She had opened them and added them. Instead of beef stew she now had beef stew soup as Nancy laughingly called it — "stone soup."

That story exemplifies Nancy's complete attitude about life. If you can laugh about it, you can cope with it. When we were kids that was her attitude, and it is still with her today. She has a wonderful, wonderful way of looking at things now, and she did then. She is my Nancy with the laughing face, a good friend in my childhood, and one I reclaimed this past weekend when I once again went really home.

'Old' Card Makes Him Wonder

Last summer I got a postcard from friends vacationing in St. Petersburg, Fla. It read, "Conjugate the verb old: I is old. You is old. We is all old." Lately I find myself remembering that card and thinking I is old. Not that I think I am ready for the retirement home or anything like that. I just wonder how I got to be in my 40s when my mind is still thinking it is in its 20s.

When I was home recently in South Carolina and saw some of my friends from childhood, I thought they really looked older, and so must I. And when I look at my father now, I see that he has gotten beyond middle age into old age, and I wonder when that happened.

When I was small, I thought I would stay young forever. Everybody of importance was under 20. Or at least under 25. I honestly remember wondering how it must feel to be 40. My mother died when she was 40, and I thought at the time she had had a rich and full life. A few weeks ago I marked the anniversary of her death. It has been 31 years. She would have been 71, and had she lived all this time and died it still would have been too soon.

I don't worry as much about looking old as feeling old. If my mind and body can stay alert and usable it will be fine. I find now that my heroes are those people who continue to function and function well as they become 70, 80 and 90. Katherine Hepburn is almost 80 and is still an actress and an author. George Abbott is over 100 and he is still producing Broadway plays. Bette Davis has survived a stroke and other ailments and still seeks new projects. These have become my heroes.

Maybe I got so morbid about age because the mother of one of my close friends died last week. I went to her funeral in South Carolina. I hate funerals, but for some friends I make the effort and go. But I don't participate in visits to see open caskets. Like Eve of the three faces, my personality would be shattered by such an event.

Anyway I went to the funeral of my friend's mother. It pointed out to how badly these things can be handled. First off the organist was strictly cut rate. She had been provided by the funeral home and must have been the mortician's daughter. I didn't recognize a single hymn she played, and we were supposed to know them. Each interlude she played caused more pain and sorrow than the event we were attending.

Secondly the ceremony was conducted by my friend's ex-father in law. This minister had never liked my friend, but out of love for his grandchildren he conducted the ceremony. It was almost through gritted teeth that he mentioned the son of the dear departed. By this time I was on the verge of hysteria. Laughing in church has always been a fear of mine. Howling at a funeral was a nightmare come true.

When I found out that the poor lady could not be laid to rest in the plot that had been dug for her, I thought I had ventured forth into the twilight zone. For some reason a distant relative had arrived on the scene and claimed the sacred spot of plot—after it had been dug. The matter could not be resolved in time for the grave side service so it had to be canceled, and this got every tongue to wagging and the gossip buzzing.

My friend and I gathered at his motel room a few hours after the ceremony and laughed together over the ritual that had existed. This was not meant out of disrespect for his mother but for the foibles of people who pick the most inopportune times to show their pettiness. Everyone would say they would never act that way, but somehow there is always someone who does.

After we had had our laugh, my friend made the comment that now he was an orphan. That jolted the laughs out of my system. He was no longer anyone's child. There was no buffer between him and the grave. He was the oldest generation for his line of the family. That was a shock and one that has stuck with me.

So now I am thinking about getting old. I guess it will pass. These things usually do. But one thing I won't forget. As we were leaving the church after the funeral was completed someone came up to me and grabbed me in a tight embrace. "Tommy Cooper," she said. (Tommy is my older brother's name) "It is so good to see you." And turning to my wife, she added. "And is this your daughter?"

I is old. You is old. My wife is young—but not young enough to be my daughter!

School Memories Teach Lessons

They are all heading back to school. You see their fresh faces and their ever-developing personalities as they head through the doors of the school buildings and start another year of learning and living. The youth of America have ended their summer days and are back to school daze.

School years stay with us throughout our lives. At any given moment a flash of a memory can crowd our minds and pop full blown into our consciousness. One that continues to haunt me is a time when I was starting the fourth grade. I was always ambiguous about the start of school. I liked getting back to see people, but I didn't like ending my summer routine. Plus I was always a little anxious about how it would all go.

My mother used to walk me to school on the first day of class. That was to make sure she met my teacher and that I was comfortable with my surroundings. But going into the fourth grade I decided I was too big to have her accompany me. I went that first day by myself!

I remember going into the classroom and finding my seat. I was one of the first to get there. The teacher had not even come into the room. Several kids came in whom I did not recognize. They looked at me, and I looked at them. Then the teacher came in. She looked at me, and I looked at her. "Jackie," she said, "I enjoyed teaching you last year, but I don't think you want to be in third grade again."

Yes, I had gone back to my old seat in the third grade. Old habits die hard for me, and the pull of security had brought me back there. I could have died when I realized what I had done. Not only did I have to flee from that room, but by the time I got to my fourth grade class all the best seats had been taken. It was a day and an event I will never forget. I was mortified by it as only a fourth grader can be, and of course it became a legendary story that lives at Florida Street School in Clinton, S.C. to this day.

Another incident I remember from my school daze occurred in the ninth grade. I was nominated for vice president of my class. One of my opponents was Sandra Ray. Sandra was then and stayed one of the prettiest girls in our class. She was stiff competition. She was also well brought up and polite. We all were.

After the first ballot it was a tie between Sandra and me. There had to be a run off. I was sweating bullets. I wanted to be vice president of the class, and I am sure Sandra did too. Anyway after we had voted at school that day, and we were leaving school, Sandra came up to me and said she had voted for me. I said I had voted for her. One of us was lying. I hadn't voted for Sandra. I had voted for me.

In that time and at that age the proper thing to do was to vote for your opponent. Still for some reason that didn't make sense to me. If I was going to run for something, I must think that I was the best. That was my logic. That is why I cast my vote for me.

I won vice president. I won by one vote. Sandra and I had both voted for a winner. If I had voted for Sandra that would have been one less vote for me and one more vote for her. She would have won by one vote. I would have lost.

That was the first time I ever voted for myself but not the last. From that point on I realized that in any race you should be able to count on yourself. So if you ever see Jackie Cooper running for something you know he will get at least one vote—his own.

That vote of confidence was one of the greatest lessons I learned in high school, a place where most of the important lessons of life are learned. So students of today listen to Uncle Jackie. (1) Always remember when you have been promoted, and (2) always vote for yourself. If you don't deserve your vote then stay out of the race.

The Unknown Sometimes Hurts Worse

It has become acceptable to think, remember, and write about Vietnam. It has taken many years for America to be able to face this scar on the face of our history, but for everything there is a season, and the '80s are the season for remembering.

My college years and the war in Vietnam collided. I managed to make it through college and law school, but the omnipresent draft was there beside me. The day after I was admitted to the South Carolina Bar I was sworn into the Air Force. My military career had begun, and it was a good one.

For four years I served Uncle Sam at Robins Air Force Base. Many of my friends and acquaintances went to Vietnam. Some volunteered while others were ordered there. I would have gone if I was ordered, but only if I was ordered. A Vietnam volunteer I was not.

In truth Vietnam was mostly a haze to me. Being in an Air Force town, I was spared the anti-military sentiments of parts of the country. The war was a distant event that bordered my life but did not intrude upon it. EXCEPT –

Chris Macintyre was a farm boy. He loved the outdoors and all animals. He was truly a good person. He and I went to school together, but he was a couple of years behind me. But our school was small enough that you could get to know just about everybody who went there.

Chris was popular, immensely so. He had the natural ability to make everyone feel special who came into contact with him. Sometimes I thought he was too good to be true, but I could never prove it. He loved life, he lived life, he made other people's lives better.

Everyone in Clinton, S.C. said Chris was really going to go places. His parents who were just good hard-working people could hardly contain their pride. Chris was the apple of their eyes and the delight of their souls. He was a gift from God who got better each and every day he was alive.

Chris sailed through high school, and he graduated with honors. He was the president of the student body and was voted "Most Popular" in the senior class. The honors continued as he decided on college. West Point was offered, and he accepted. There he also excelled.

I saw Chris off and on during those college years. We would hit up in Clinton at the same time and would catch up on each others' lives. We never discussed Vietnam much. Maybe we thought if we didn't talk about it, it would just go away. It didn't.

I was in law school when Chris graduated from West Point. He came home. Clinton always held an attraction for him that it didn't for me. I wanted to see California. Cliff wanted to see his parents' farm. I wanted to explore the bright lights. Chris wanted to see the beauty of nature again. Even with all of his potential I think he could have lived on that farm in Clinton forever and been happy.

It didn't shock me when I heard Chris had volunteered for Vietnam. That was just like him. If he was going to do something, he was going to do it right. And since the military had given him a good education he was going to give them the best he had to offer. That meant taking his turn in Vietnam.

Chris went to Vietnam, and after he had been there for less than a month he disappeared. He went out in a helicopter on some mission and just disappeared. That smiling face just slipped away into the jungles of Vietnam.

Chris Macintyre has never returned to Clinton. No explanation of his fate has ever been offered. His parents know no peace. To this day they wait, and hope and pray.

The war in Vietnam was a haze to me. It took place over the waters, in another land, in another world. But the loss of Chris was real. Like his parents I wonder what really happened to him. And like his parents I still wonder if there isn't some chance he is still alive. In a bizarre way that is the worst hurt of all.

Some Parties Are Memorable

As I am writing this, I am also celebrating my birthday. Yes, the year has passed by once again, and I am now a year older. Where does the time go? I guess it is a true sign of aging when the years begin to fly by at the speed of sound.

Now I am not a big believer in birthday celebrations. The less said the better. I have always been this way. Even as a child I just wanted to get the gifts and let the rest of it go. No birthday parties for me. The family was quite enough.

There was one kid in my class who always had a big birthday weekend party. Every year we all had to go trooping out to his house in the country to spend a whole weekend. I hated it. I dreaded his birthday more than mine. It meant a whole weekend of sleeping on the floor, eating food I didn't like, and not going to the bathroom. I never participated in non-familiar bathrooms.

Maybe that is what soured me on birthday parties at an early age. I really don't like anything that puts the spotlight on me completely. Now I will hog the spotlight at someone else's party but just don't have me responsible for everybody's good times and happiness.

The best party ever given for me almost was the worst. It was when I was moving to California. Friends of mine said they were going to give a goodbye party at Robins Air Force Base and invite everyone. It was going to be the party to end all parties. I was in mortal fear of what would occur.

My best friends also know that I have a fear of throwing a party and nobody coming. Call it stupidity or call it insecurity, but it is a real fear of mine. Well this party was going to have a hundred or more people. At least that is the way it started.

The week before the main event people started calling to apologize for the fact they were not going to be there. There was a lot going on so I knew there would be some dropouts, but this was a mass exodus. The organizers of the party acted a little embarrassed but maintained their composure. There were still 90 people coming, then 80, then 70 and so on.

On the day of the gala we were down to about 26, and we weren't sure of them. I was physically ill. Each time I called my wife I reported another drop out. I mean these were some of my true-blue friends who had last minute emergencies and were not going to show. I had begun to make my revenge list.

Finally the time for the party was at hand. I was nobly acting like it all didn't matter and that I was thrilled 18 people were going to be there to see us off. Plus there was a lot of food that had been ordered and could not be sent back so we all would be well fed.

Into the Officer's Club I went and headed for the back room. When I opened the door, I was in shock. The place was jammed with people. It had to be more than the 100 I originally thought would be there. I had been tricked and tricked royally. Everyone had been in on the joke but me.

People, I learned, had had to go out of the room where I was when I was told about another no show. I had looked so pathetic and drab it had been impossible not to laugh at me. Plus, they couldn't believe that with such a list of excuses I didn't catch on. Dumb, naive me. I bought it all. I believed it all.

Still, what a party it was. It was the best ever. I had been so prepared for the worst that I could really enjoy the best. I moved to California on the wings of friendship and love.

To this day I don't like parties, especially ones for me. But in my mind I will always remember that "going away" party as the best ever. I expected the worst and had the best. I will never forget it. Even when I have 40 more birthdays it will still be fresh in my mind.

Memories of Good Times Can Brighten Dark Days

Americans are funny people. We get depressed if things are going good, and we get depressed if things are going badly. We spend half our lives fighting to succeed, and then are miserable if we do because we have no more mountains left to conquer. What a mess we make out of our emotional lives, and what a pity, in most instances, we do it to ourselves.

All my life I have heard people say you have to have the bad times in order to appreciate the good. I have always hated that concept, but I guess now that I am older I have to admit it is true. Most people do not really appreciate life until they have faced a tragedy or a near tragedy.

Just recently I was talking with a lady whose husband had an aneurysm burst in his brain. Thank God, he is recovering steadily now, but it was touch and go for a while. This lady says it has changed her total outlook on life. No longer do the little things bother her. She has learned that life can be fleeting and the good times are to be cherished.

Her husband is being treated at Emory, and she says you ought to see the tragedies that people deal with every day. While visiting her husband, she got a first-hand view. It will sober your thoughts in a minute. After talking a while with this lady, I realize the general complaints of myself and others are nothing but spoiled whining of the most juvenile kind.

It is like the people who complain after they have a child if it was not of a certain sex. Those statements really make my blood boil. There are so many, many couples who would give anything just to have a baby regardless of the sex. But no, some of us get upset if we didn't get the "carry the name on" son or the petite daughter.

I think it is so funny that in most instances it is the man who gets his nose out of shape over the baby's sex when he is the one who determines the sex with his genes. If you want to blame someone, buddy, blame yourself.

Yes, people do tend to sit around and ask themselves if this is as good as life gets. As Peggy Lee sang in the song several, several years ago, "Is that all there is?" What do we want there to be!

Three years ago this month my wife discovered a lump on the side of her neck. The doctor said he was sure it was just an enlarged lymph node, but he needed to do surgery just to make sure. I fell apart. My mother died of lymphatic cancer, and I just did not think I could face another battle of that type again.

My wife and I clung to each other for the days while we waited for the surgery to be performed. Then we sweated out the lab report which came back benign. Benign has to be the sweetest word in the English language.

From that time on I have said to any and all who will listen, if the problems I have are money problems then I am OK. The things that worry me are the things that can't be fixed by money. That is when I feel helpless and afraid.

After we got that report, and after I got my wife home, and when I had her and my two boys healthy and happy in my home, well, that is when I knew that this is as good as it gets. And for me that is more than enough.

Service Once Came with the Sale

A few days ago I went into a grocery store to pick up a jar of spaghetti sauce. Unable to locate the aisle on which it could be found, I asked a young woman who had on a sign identifying herself as a checker at that store where could I find it.

"I just work here. I don't shop here," she answered.

So much for checker courtesy and customer appreciation. And so much for my visits to that store ever again. If the management can't inspire more loyalty in their personnel than that, they don't deserve my business. And if that young lady doesn't have more pride in the work she does, I predict a long hard life for her.

Now I know from first hand experience that working in a grocery store is not the fun job of the century. At least back in the '50s when I was the stockboy, bag carrier at Johnson Brothers Supermarket in Clinton, S.C., it wasn't. But I survived it, and I never told anybody that "I just work here, I don't shop here."

That is because just about everybody in Clinton shopped for something at Johnson's. Black, white, purple and green — they all came in the store and on a regular basis. I worked there on Friday afternoon and Saturdays, and I didn't need a clock to tell me what time it was; I could tell by who was in the store.

Albert Johnson was the brother I knew the best. He handled the front of the store where I worked. His brother Robert ran the meat market in the back. Plus, Robert cooked barbecue outside from time to time – it was the best in South Carolina. But Albert and I ran the front of the store with help from Robert Lee, the jack-of-all-trades and Shirley, the checkout lady.

I started working at Johnson's when I was 13-years-old. In my family that was the age when you got work. I thought it was too young then, and I think of it as too young now. My gosh, you are only young once so why start to work so early? For most of us once we start, it is for the rest of our lives.

But this was 1954, and Albert and Robert had offered my Daddy a job for me. I was paid 50 cents an hour. I worked four hours on Fridays and 11 hours on Saturday which meant I collected $7.50 on Saturday night at eight p.m.. At least I should have collected that amount.

I was a skinny kid back then and could eat from dawn till dusk and never gain an ounce. And I loved to eat what I loved to eat. Most of that which I loved was junk food, and Johnson's offered me an abundant source of such food.

Pepsi's flowed down my throat, and potato chips crunched in my teeth. And for the piece de resistance there was always the wonderful Pet strawberry pie that was made with real strawberries and ice cream. I would put one in the freezer and eat on it all day Saturday.

As a result of this pigging out, I always ended up in debt on Saturday night. My father would come to pick me up, and he would ask Albert how much he owed for me. I was bought and sold every Saturday night.

The funny thing was my father would never complain. I guess just the fact that I was working and staying out of trouble was enough. Johnson Brothers was babysitting me in a sense, and he only had to pay the difference between what I ate and what they paid.

I worked at Johnson's until I graduated from high school. I never did learn to love the work, but I did learn to love the people who came in there. I still see them now when I go back to Clinton. Not at Johnson's. The store has been torn down and the employees dispersed. Albert died a few years back and Robert is retired. Shirley is still a good friend of mine, and we laugh over some of the times we had together at Johnson's. Robert Lee just disappeared.

Maybe the girl who told me she "just worked at the grocery store" and didn't shop there, should concentrate on the people she meets in her work rather than the work itself. It might make a difference to her. If that doesn't work she should try eating up all of her salary. That is bound to make her feel better. It always did with me.

This is a Tall Turkey Story

When I was growing up in South Carolina if you were going to have a pet you had a dog. Nobody had a cat for a pet. I never wanted one then and thought I would never want one now. But somehow we did end up with a cat, and now I am a confirmed cat person.

The other day I went to a friend's house who had a cocker spaniel. That is the kind of dog I had when I was younger. They have always been my favorite kind of dog. But I have gotten older, and dogs have gotten rowdier. This dog was absolutely hysterical. It bit, growled, licked smiled, ran around in circles and bounced off the walls. I think the dog was on speed.

Now a cat would never do that. At least my cat Fluff wouldn't. She would never want to appear that anxious to please. She might allow you to scratch her head, but she would never appear or act overly familiar.

But back to the dogs of my youth. They too were a little hyper, but then so was I. My dogs were called Madam and Lady. Madam was Lady's mother. My family had had two previous cocker spaniels when I was real young, but they were now both buried under the pine tree in our backyard. One died with distemper, and one was run over by a car

Madam and Lady were semi-house dogs. We had a fenced-in backyard, but they stayed in the house a lot. My mother liked dogs and liked having them around. The rest of us did too, but she had the deciding vote.

So the dogs were generally in the house or in the backyard. They did not roam free in the neighborhood. Not intentionally. But there were always the times when my brother or I would open the front door, and they would take off up the street or down through our neighbors' yards. My brother and I would have to chase them, and when they got tired they would stop and let us bring them home. They thought it was a game.

One night it was cold and rainy. The weather was not fit for man nor beast. But my dogs didn't know that. Somebody opened the front door, and they were off like a shot. It was dark, it was raining, it was awful. By the time we got coats on to go look for them they could not be found. We searched for hours, but couldn't find them. Finally we gave up and just hoped they would come on home.

The next morning when I left for school, they still weren't home. I was afraid they were gone forever. I confided my heartbreak to my almost girlfriend Mary Ann. She lived three blocks up the street from me. Her father was the chief of police. They had a big house and yard. They also had animals in their back yard — turkey animals. They weren't supposed to have animals like these within the city limits, but when you are chief of police, you can do things like that.

Anyway as I told my tale of woe to Mary Ann, she said she knew where my dogs were. They were at her house. I rushed into the school to call my mother and tell her. She and my father went to get the dogs. They were at Mary Ann's house all right. They had been found that morning by Mary Ann's parents in a pile of turkey feathers. They had decided to celebrate Thanksgiving early, and had killed but not eaten 14 turkeys.

Mary Ann never became my girlfriend. My father and the chief of police had heated negotiations over recompense for the turkeys. The city ordinance which prohibited animals such as turkeys from being raised in the city limits became a hot topic in my hometown. But I got to keep my dogs. My parents saw the whole incident as something that was not their fault. They were just following their instincts. My folks were great about stuff like that.

Madam died before I entered college, and Lady only lived a few months after I went away to school. I haven t owned a dog since then. Now I own a cat who hates turkey. It's one of the reasons I love her like I do.

You <u>Can</u> Always Come Home

Last week I had a letter from some friends who are living up north now. They used to live in Perry, but his work required the family to pack up and move away. The letter was full of remarks about the good old days and the fun we had when they lived in Perry. It also stated they were clinging to the fact that I had moved my family to California and had brought them back to Perry.

As you can tell, my friends want to come home. They have been through a winter of snow and ice and they want the southern comforts back again. At least when I uprooted my family, I took them to a warm climate. Regardless of the job, there is very little that would induce me to move to the tundras of our country.

No, I chose California, a place where I had always wanted to live. We stayed there for two years, and then we moved back. We were lucky. I got my California experience out of my system, and we got to move back to the same town we had left.

Moving to a new place is never easy. No matter how big an adventure you are expecting, leaving friends and family behind is a problem. In our case we left some of our best friends ever in Perry, plus we left our children's grandparents in Florida and South Carolina feeling like the end of the world had come.

I should add that no one, friend nor family, shared my enthusiasm about moving to California. They all knew that those people out there are really weird. I didn't worry about the people, I only worried about the earthquakes

California wasn't paradise on earth. We had a lot of adjustments to make. In Perry we had sometimes felt people knew too much about our business. In California nobody cared at all. We got a new car while we were out there, and it took over a month for anyone to notice. And then it was to wonder why we didn't get a Volvo.

Attending church was also a different experience in California. We tried to be Baptists again to satisfy our parents who will never figure out why we turned Methodist. The Baptists in California just didn't seem the same as the Baptists in the South. The minister was having an affair with a member of our Sunday School class, and nobody seemed very upset about it. So we moved on to the Methodist Church.

In the Methodist Church we met our pastor, Mr. Hughes. He looked to be in his late 60s. Later we met a lady named Mary Beth Hughes, she was in her 20s. We thought she must be the pastor's daughter. We were wrong; it was his wife. He was divorced from wife number one; this was wife number two.

One of the members of the church, who had been there for quite some time, explained that they allowed their pastors one divorce. Two and they were out. They were more conservative than the Baptists.

As I got to know the minister, I liked him better and better. He had been a theater arts major in college and always went to the movies on Sunday after his sermons were over. That's my kind of preacher. He also used his theatrics in the church. The altar was in the round, and Mr. Hughes would put on a cordless mike and ramble about through the congregation while he preached. It was especially effective when he did the sermon on the mount from memory.

One thing I couldn't accept while we were out there was that there was no Sunday School during the summer. Mr. Hughes explained to me that people were just so busy with the many outdoor activities available; they just wouldn't come to Sunday School. I balked at that, and we formed a summer Sunday School class, and it was well attended. It was still going strong when we moved back to Georgia.

I wrote back to my faraway friends this week. I told them to look on the positive side of their new home. Think of the new experiences they were gaining. Think of the new friends they were making. I encouraged them to get involved in their new community. And I also told them they should move back to Perry at the first opportunity.

Thomas Wolfe was wrong. You can go home again, and you should. If you are happy where you are, then stay. And if you sometimes, by mistake, leave it, then don't be afraid to admit your error and come on home. Life is too short to be miserable. There is always another job and another opportunity if you look for it.

Names Aren't Carved in Rock

I was talking with a group of friends a few days ago, and the subject of names came up. It is amazing to hear how parents have decided upon the names they have given their children. One woman said she named her daughter Candy because she had craved candy all during her pregnancy. Another said if that had been the case she would have named her daughter "squash" since that was what she had craved.

Well my parents named me Jackie after my mother's brother. He was named Aubrey, but his nickname was Jack. Don't ask me why, it just was one of those funny things of life. Of course, I would prefer to be called Jack if my name had been Aubrey.

Anyway on my birth certificate my name is spelled out to be J-a-c-k-i-e. It is not John or Jack, it is Jackie. I stress that because all of my life people have been trying to shorten it to Jack. I have resisted that change forever and will continue till it is carved on my tombstone. One reason I have resisted the diminution of my name is to spite my brother.

When we were growing up in Clinton, S.C., he was Tommy and I was Jackie. But the first week he went off to

Furman University in Greenville, S.C., he wrote back home and signed the letter "Tom." It made me want to throw up. If he had been Tommy for 18 years, I didn't know why he had to change at this late date.

A few months later he compounded his error in my eyes. He changed it again, this time to "Thom." Okay so his name is really Thomas, and it logically follows that Thom could be his name. But whoever heard of anybody being called Thom. The only one I knew was that shoe guy "Thom McCan."

So this change in my brother's name cemented my determination to never be known as Jack. But I did change my name to other names during my younger years. I spent a whole summer being known at summer camp as "Rock Dixon." This was back in the pre-AIDS days when Rock Hudson was an enviable screen hunk. And there was a great football player in South Carolina by the name of King Dixon. So I fused the two and became Rock Dixon.

It is amazing what the change of a name can do. For that summer I was an entirely different personality than my normal one. I lived life with a swagger. I attracted more girls than ever before, and they would giggle and flirt and call me "Rocky." That is what girls do around a guy named Rock Dixon.

My charade as Rock Dixon was possible because I was spending the weeks of the summer at church camp, and everyone in my group went along with it. How I convinced them to do that is a mystery to me, but they did. But when I got back to Clinton, Rock was retired.

Oh I still got letters from some of the girls which were sent to Rock Dixon at my home address, which caused some confusion at the post office and with my parents. Somehow I talked my way out of it by saying it was a guy I met at camp who liked a girl, and I was forwarding the letters on to him. It didn't make sense then, and it sure doesn't make sense now, but somehow they bought it.

I still think about my Rock Dixon days from time to time. And I can still feel the difference I felt by being that somebody else. But down deep I knew then, and I know now, that I am really Jackie Cooper. Rock Dixon was cool, but he was very superficial. And I can't imagine what he would have been as an adult. Still sometimes in the dull periods of my life I get the urge to go to a new town and try it out and see.

Mail Brings Nice Surprises

Recently I saw a survey concerning people's contentment with the U.S. Postal Service. It showed that appreciation and trust of the postal system is at an all time high. And I can certainly understand why. Even with all of our complaints about how expensive it is getting to mail a letter, you still have to be in awe of the amount of mail that is moved around this country and the timely manner in which it is done.

Now that the Christmas season is upon us once again, it is time to appreciate the mailman/woman more than ever. People we have not heard from all year long will get the urge to tell us what they are doing with their lives by mailing a Christmas card. Plus we might even get pictures of them and their children if we are lucky.

I have always been fascinated by what may be arriving in the mail. It is like a lottery. You never know when somebody might just decide to send you a check. Or you might hear from somebody you have been thinking about. It is, like the telephone, something that has all the potential for surprise.

My family knows that going to get the mail from our mailbox is one of the little joys of my life. When we go off on a trip, I always look forward to going to the box and seeing what goodies are in store for me. It is part of my daily ritual. I will even pick up mail for other people if they wish.

Some of my friends only go to the Post Office to check their box once or twice a week. This amazes me. How do they know there isn't something vitally important waiting for them there? And you know if it is a surprise, it is going to be a good one. Bad news never comes by mail. The phone is used for that.

My enjoyment of the mail dates back to my childhood (I can hear the groans out there as you turn to each other and say - he's going back to his childhood again!) When I was growing up our mail was delivered by J.D. McKee. Summer, winter, spring and fall as well as heat, rain or storm, J.D. brought the mail to us.

He always hit our house at the same time. We lived at the bottom of a hill. I would go out at one p.m. each day (this was before I was in school or during summer vacation) and start looking up the hill for him. Almost on the dot he would round the corner and make his way to me, house by house.

When he got to my house, he would always have some piece of mail for me. Maybe it was an advertisement or a magazine, or some stamps I had ordered. But it was always something. It was wonderful. I could always count on J.D. to pull something from his bag that was meant for me. It was almost miraculous.

J.D. looked like somebody who could and would work miracles. He stood well over 6 feet, and he had a voice that was resonant. I say that from my vantage point now, but back then it was just deep and booming. But it always made me think that if I ever heard the voice of God that was how it would sound.

J.D. was active in our church and seemed to epitomize what was good in the world. I never saw him angry or flustered, never saw him tired or emotional. He was just the calmest, most level person I ever knew. And when you are six and seven you can just sense goodness in someone, and I sensed it in him.

Some modern changes in the world I think are better. Some are worse. The postman who delivers the mail on our street now drives a postal vehicle and never gets out of it. He just sticks the mail in the boxes and moves on. My kids don't know his name, or for that matter, neither do I.

I still enjoy waiting for the mail to come, or in my case now, waiting for it to be put in the boxes in the post office. The excitement remains. But I do miss the days of J.D.. He never disappointed that sense of goodness I felt. And through him the post office and the mail service are something I respect.

Physicals Make Him Sick

Today I had my yearly physical, or in my case the every other year physical. I always plan to have a physical once a year, but somehow the time gets by, and it is one, two, or maybe even three years before I get around to it.

Usually when I decide to have it, it is because I have developed a symptom of some kind which I think indicates an early death. Yes, I am a hypochondriac. I fear illness as much as I do airplanes. I call it the dying/flying fear.

Back to my latest trauma. For weeks prior to my examination I had a headache. It came and went like the tides. Some would call it sinus trouble. I called it a tumor. I just knew it was lurking inside my brain causing my pain. The fact that aspirin made it go away did not assuage my fears.

But the weekend before the physical my wife and I went away to Brunswick and Jekyll Island. Maybe it was the sea water or maybe it was the lack of stress, but the headache went away. So now I had a scheduled physical with no symptoms. Oh well, I was sure the doctor would find something.

Came the day of the physical and I dressed in my cleanest underwear. My mother had raised me right. Doctors don't want to see dirty underwear when they attend you in a car wreck or when they give you a physical. I'm sure they notice, don't you?

The first thing I had to do at the doctor's office was give blood. Well, that was the second thing I had to give. When the nurse tried to find a vein they were all in hiding. Not only do I have rolling veins, I also have collapsible veins. You hit them, they spurt out a minute amount of blood and then collapse. Usually I do too.

Somehow we drilled for blood and got a gusher. The drawer should get an award. So should the drawee. Neither I nor my veins collapsed.

Soon I had gone through all the tests. The doctor told me to have a seat in the waiting room, and we would talk when he had gotten the results. You should never give me time to think in a doctor's waiting room. I sat there and tried to read the paper. I looked at the date on the paper. I wondered if it would be the day I got the BAD news.

They called my name, and I went back to the doctor's office. He led me to a seat and shut the door behind me. I was sure that was to keep the people in the other offices from hearing my screams when he gave me the BAD news.

The doctor flipped my chest X-rays on the screen behind the desk. I was sure I saw dark areas lurking there. Was that a tumor? I dared not ask. "Looks clear, don't you think?" he asked.

I wanted to reply, "Who's paying who for what here?" But I only nodded and waited for the real revelation to come. There was none. He gave me a clean bill of health. Life was renewed.

That was the good part. The better part was he didn't complain about my weight. If he didn't mention it then I figure it must be OK. Doctors always tell you if you weigh too much. He might as well have said, "Eat your heart out, Cooper."

I left his office and gained ten pounds before I got back to mine. It is going to be a very good year. But wait a minute, what is this burning feeling in my chest? I guess some would call it heartburn, but I know better. I have advanced stomach rot, and he just didn't want to tell me.

Is there a doctor reading this? Well don't look now but you just got yourself a new patient. I'll bring my X-rays with me.

Miracles Happen at the Movies

This is a story for people who believe in miracles, and for those who don't. It is a true story, and it has as its cast of characters: Miss Georgia, a Santa named Spielberg, two elves named Kelly and Levy, and an assortment of kids in all shapes and sizes. The miracle, as I like to think of it, happened in Georgia during the Christmas season, the season when miracles are most likely to happen.

The start of the incidents which were to lead up to the miracle began several months ago. A friend of mine named Kelly Jerles had been crowned Miss Georgia. She had entered the contest as Miss Marietta, a place where the people are friendly and know a pretty face when they see one.

Kelly and I have been friends for a long time, so when she asked me if I would be a judge in the 1988 Miss Marietta Pageant I was happy to oblige. Little did I know that I was being sent to that city for a purpose.

One of my fellow judges was a lady named Pam Carter. She has been active in Miss Georgia events for years and knows the pageant system like the back of her hand. She also is a teacher of special education in Columbus. Her students are handicapped in a variety of ways and special in a million others.

It has always amazed me that there are teachers who have the patience and the caring ways to work with handicapped people. I count them among God's angels on earth. When Pam began to talk to me about her kids, I was her fan for life.

She told me different stories about the children, and one of them really hit home. She said they all had heard about the movie "E.T." and wanted to see it. She asked me if I knew where she could get the video to show to them. I explained that "E.T." is not out on video and won't be for some time. Steven Spielberg plans to re-release it in the future, probably two to three years from now.

Pam explained that some of her kids might not be around when that re-release occurs. Some of them have illnesses that are terminal, while others have conditions that just get progressively severe.

When I got home from the pageant, I decided to write Steven Spielberg and ask him what he could do for these special children. Now Steven Spielberg and I are not pen pals, nor are we social acquaintances. But again a force more powerful than me or him was at work and my letter got to him.

In a very short time I received a call from Chris Kelly of his staff. She took down the information and said she would be working with me on it. A few weeks later a man named Marvin Levy called and said the movie would be made available. I just needed to tell him when and where.

Working with Pam, we got the Carmike Cinema chain of Columbus to provide a theater. They also furnished free refreshments for all the kids. Julie Erickson of Universal Pictures in Atlanta sent "E.T." buttons for the kids to wear. Everyone did their part and more.

On Tuesday, Dec. 15, "E.T." was shown to Pam Carter's kids. They went by bus to the theater where arrangements were made to place each kid in a comfortable position. The wheelchairs were placed in the aisles and other special arrangements were made.

None of these kids had ever been to a movie theater before. They had no idea what a motion picture was. One little boy wondered how they had gotten such a big television screen in the theater. Others were afraid when the lights were lowered so the theater people wisely kept them on a little brighter than usual.

Soon the magic of "E.T." took over. Kids who had not shown much emotion in the past were laughing, smiling, crying. "E.T."'s heartlight had made the connection once again, and the kids were repeating over and over "E.T. phone home."

Each child who was there could be the subject of a separate story, but one particularly touched me. Pam had told me about a little girl who desperately wanted to see the movie. Well, by the time arrangements were made for the showing, this little girl had lost her sight. But she came to the theater, and she listened to the sounds of "E.T." and saw the film through her heart. Her mother said it had done wonders for her just to know someone cared enough to send the film.

I didn't go to Columbus for the presentation of the film. The information I have given you was passed along to me from Pam. I didn't think it would be anything but selfish for me to go. Maybe if I could have observed them un-awares, it would have been all right, but I didn't want this to be a media event. It was their screening, their movie, their time.

Some people will say it was just a matter of me being in the right place at the right time in meeting Pam, in writing

Steven Spielberg, in all the people getting involved. I disagree. I think from the time Kelly Jerles talked to me about judging the contest in Marietta, a miracle was in the making. A miracle brought about by some kids' wishes.

Maybe some things are coincidence. Maybe some things are chance. But this Christmas I saw a miracle happen. And you will never convince me, or Pam Carter, or Kelly Jerles, or Julie Erickson, or the people at Carmike Cinemas, or Chris Kelly, or Marvin Levy, or maybe even Steven Spielberg that it was anything else.

So the next time you are hoping for what seems to be the impossible, remember "E.T." and the kids in Columbus and how he came to see them during the Christmas season of 1987.

Reflections from Route 88

Ah 1988, a year of looking back at life and love. This is the last Route of this book's journey but only one of many I am still traveling. While on route 88 I reflected on what life is, and what life can be. This is probably my most philosophical year, so read on and take the last leg of this book's journey.

Resolutions Start the New Year

Now that 1988 has gotten here, I have a very good feeling about it. This is going to be the year that I really accomplish some of my goals - the year I make some resolutions and actually make an effort to put them into effect.

One goal is to go to New York. I have been through New York on my way to Europe (I won a cruise on the Mediterranean), but I have never actually stayed in New York. People I know and respect have raved about what a great place that city is. This year I am going to find out what its secret is.

And when I go to New York, I am going to see the play "Les Miserables." I have the tape of the original Broadway cast, and it is some of the greatest music I have ever heard. How I wish I had gotten to New York to hear that original cast! But they are now scattered, and Gary Morris of country music fame's in the lead. Still, the lure of Jean Valjean is strong and I really must see that play.

A friend of mine has tickets to see "Phantom of the Opera," another Andrew Lloyd Webber hit. His tickets are for a performance in February. I would like to see that show too, but the next available tickets are for November

1988 performances. When a show is a hit on Broadway, it is a big hit.

I am also resolving to learn how to shop. All I know how to do now is purchase. My wife says there is a big difference between shopping and purchasing. In true shopping, you don't even have to make a purchase. It's the glory of the pursuit that is the prize.

My idea of buying something has always been (1) know where it is, (2) go where it is, and (3) buy it. Sweet, simple and short. Sounds good to me, but that is not the attitude that would make my spouse happy.

On our recent Christmas trip to Florida we stopped and shopped at some outlet malls. It is like visiting the grave-yard of deserted husbands. You see them all around the stores—waiting, waiting, and waiting. They are dejected, deserted, lonely men who ask only one thing of life, and that is that their wives come back to them ready to move on.

Sometimes I get the feeling that these men started off the day young and healthy but have aged and grayed sitting and waiting for the "shopping" spree to end. This must be somewhat true, as a good percentage of the men I saw were older looking. And I know that by the time my wife had finished for the day I was feeling a good ten years older.

There must be some enjoyment a male can find in this shopping adventure. It can't be a purely female sport. But try as I might, the secret of the successful shopper just eludes me. Still, this is the year I resolve to give it a better try.

My third resolution is to make this the year I stop whining. This is the sport I really enjoy. I can take whining to a higher art form. And what enjoyment it gives! You haven't had a true high in life if you haven't experienced the ultimate whine.

I can usually give a good whine about my job at the end of the day. But anybody can do that. I get better and more professional when I whine about food. I can say, "Isn't there anything here to eat?" and make it sound like my heart is breaking.

Last year, 1987, was the year of the whiner across the country. From Oliver North to Jim Bakker, from Donna Rice to Jessica Hahn, we had whiners coming at us from all directions. Every time you turned on TV, somebody was telling us about something that somebody did or didn't do to or for them. That is what prompted me to give up my whining career. There is just too much competition.

So 1988 is going to be a time of travel, shopping and non-whining for me. What are you going to do with your year?

Survival Tips for Snow – Lay In the Munchies

As I write this, the elements are going crazy, and snow is falling on Middle Georgia. Maybe the rest of the country is used to such precipitation, but when it comes to Georgia we all go a little bit crazy. Cars slide, people panic, children go wild. It is a time for fun, fear and frostbite.

As for me, I have never been a snow freak. I don't like the stuff. I don't like to be cold, and those flakes personify coldness to me. I also don't like to slip and slide when I drive. Snow, or more particularly, ice does that to our roads.

Coming home today, I started down a hill, and my car decided to slide across the road into the path of another car. Then, rather than move out of my way, the lady driving the car just stopped and waited for me to hit her. I didn't. I maneuvered my slide and hit a ditch instead. She actually looked disappointed that I didn't crash into her. Guess she had her lawsuit already planned!

When I was sliding across the road, I managed to be very coherent and scream "Oh, Noooooooooooooo!" It didn't help anything, but it sure as heck made me feel better. I also did a lot of squirming on the seat, as though I could control the car through pure body weight.

Speaking of body weight, cold weather also inspires me to eat. I guess it is reverting back to the law of the jungle because I figure I should put on more weight when it is cold to protect me in case the electricity and power go out. The more fat I have to burn up in energy, the better off I will be. So as the first flakes begin to fall, I begin to eat. Today I have already been through the double Oreos, the chocolate pinwheels, popcorn, and quarts of Diet Coke. Yes, diet. I don't want to overdo it!

Since my kids are now 12 and 15, I don't panic about them the way I did during the snow of 74. At that time, our oldest was a little over a year old. The snow came, and I could just imagine it covering our house and our baby. I stocked up with enough baby food to feed all of Gerber's kids. Then I got enough Pampers to cover all their bottoms. I was a good scout. I was prepared. Tom Selleck would have been proud.

Still, I worried about the power going off and our being stranded in an apartment slowly going colder. So I put the baby in bed with us. Body heat, you know. There we were, snuggled together and warm as toast. We were ready for the worst. But, of course, the worst didn't come. The next day the sun came out, and Georgia's idea of a blizzard was gone.

I wonder how the people who live up north survive. Just imagine driving in snow and ice six or seven months a year. How do they do it? I have to say, though, that I have talked with people from Minnesota and the Dakotas, and they say they would not live anywhere else. I guess it is all what you are used to.

But for me and my house, we prefer our winters with temperatures in the mid-60s, and with only soft rain as precipitation. My idea of a winter wonderland is Jekyll Island with a cool breeze. Now, though, I am snowed in at my home in Perry. The snow and the plunging temperatures are raging outside, but I am coping. As long as the ice cream and the munchies last, so will I.

Cycle of Life and Death Goes On and On

Over the Christmas holidays I got two calls from friends. Actually, I got more than two calls from friends, but these two to which I am referring were out of the ordinary. One was a call to tell me a friend from a few years back had died. The other was a call from a more recent friend to tell me he and his wife are expecting their first child. Life and death, death and life, the cycle keeps repeating itself over and over.

The friend who died had cancer. If there is a disease I hate more than any other, it is cancer. It has taken away too many of my family and friends. I pray to God that I will see it eliminated in my lifetime.

My friend, I was told, had had a fast-acting type of cancer that spread rapidly through his body—but not so rapidly that he did not know what was happening. He knew it, and he accepted it. And he elected to die with dignity. I did not understand what that phrase means, but it was explained to me that it meant he did not want to have his life maintained by artificial means.

So my friend chose to exert control over his life and control, in a sense, over his death. I respect him for it and understand it. And for him, it was right. What I would do in the same situation, I do not know. If it was a loved one of mine, I think I would probably fight death by any means available. I say that now. What I would actually do, I hope I never have to find out.

In the telephone conversation, I learned that the funeral was more a celebration of life than of death. I can always feel that way when I know the person who died had a strong religious faith and shared my belief in an afterlife. This man had one of the strongest faiths I have ever known, which served him in life, in death, and I am sure in Heaven.

That phone conversation was both good and bad.

So was the call from my friend, the expectant father. He was full of excitement, apprehension and fear--all the normal emotions expectant parents go through (or at least the ones I did).

After rattling around for a while about the baby, my friend turned honest and said, "You know this baby was not my idea. I don't even know if I really want a baby or not." Now there was a great feeling to have, with a baby already on the way! I could tell this was going to turn into a long conversation.

As we scratched away the layers of guilt that inhibit honest conversation, we found the reason my friend was apprehensive about having a child was that he was not crazy about all children. There was a problem I could warm up to easily.

I related that when my wife and I married I had felt the same way. Other people's kids bugged the stew out of me, almost without exception. I finally decided it was because I had no control over them. When they acted like brats and their parents refused to correct them, it drove me nuts.

Then, I told my friend, my own children came along; and they, of course, were and are wonderful. They are two of my best friends and two of the greatest joys of my life. I couldn't imagine being any happier with them. And I assured him that he will feel the same way. He and his wife will find that the presence of a baby will magnify the happiness they already have – most of the time.

My friend and his wife have a good marriage. That is why I am glad they are having a child. I think children make a good marriage better and a bad marriage worse. Those idiots who say they are having a child to try to save a marriage are crazy. If a marriage is already bad, then the pressure of a baby is going to blow the lid off.

My friend bought what I said. He seemed to agree. He said it made sense. I hope it did. Sometimes I sound wise when I am really just full of hot air, but sometimes I luck out and really know what I am talking about. These latter times are few and far between, but with this call I think he hit me at the right time.

So I had two telephone calls that covered the span of life and death. Both concerned love, both concerned faith, and both concerned hope.

Memories Are Dividends of Experiences Invested

When I was a little boy, my parents decided to start their own business. My father was already a soft drink salesman, and my mother worked at a dress shop downtown, but they needed something else—something that was theirs. So they opened a grocery store.

Why not? If it didn't make any money, at least it would provide us with cheap groceries.

I marvel now at their courage in starting a business that, to my knowledge, neither of them knew anything about. Both were high school graduates, but neither had had any college courses in management nor business. They just knew what they wanted to do, and they did it.

Luckily, when they had bought the lot to build our home, it had been a double lot. Now they had room to build "the store" on that second lot. And build it they did — a concrete block building with a big sign in front that said "Cooper's Grocery."

The store had everything from soft drinks to canned goods to comic books to a kerosene pump. And it had customers — not a lot of customers, but enough to keep it going. I never knew how much money the store actually made, but I knew enough about it to be glad my dad never quit the Pepsi-Cola truck route he ran.

We only operated the store for about four years, but those were wonderful times. Being on a corner lot, it was a natural place for people to congregate. There were always people there just to talk and eat some crackers and drink soft drinks. In the summer we would sit in lawn chairs behind the back door of the store and visit. In winter we all gathered around a little gas heater and kept warm.

When I was in grammar school, I wanted to know where my mother was as soon as I got home. Before we got the store, I would start hollering for her at the top of the hill that led to our house and keep hollering until I came through the door and found her. If she wasn't there, I kept hollering her name as I went to every house in the neighborhood. After we got the store, I always knew where she would be.

A lot of our customers at the store were black, and I guess that is what built my barrier against any feelings of bigotry I could have developed later in my life. Two of my favorite people were Aunt Ida and Aunt Lula.

Aunt Ida was a giant of a woman, with only two teeth in front. She walked with a cane which she would use to shoo children and animals out of her way. She knew an endless array of stories and would tell them to us for hour after hour as she sat in the store.

Aunt Lula was a smaller person. She was more fragile, but had the reputation of being the smartest woman in the black community. She had bright piercing eyes that saw everything. And when she spoke, everybody listened—probably even E. F. Hutton.

For some reason, they liked me a lot. And I, of course, loved them totally. When they were around, I never worried about anything. The combination of Lula and Ida would scare off the devil himself.

At the store we kept a running tally of paper slips which had names printed on the back. These were the tickets for food that people bought. We had a box full of them. Some were eventually paid off, and others never were. Aunt Lula and Aunt Ida paid off some of theirs by baby-sitting with my brother and me. It was the barter system in action.

Also, there was a little girl who would come to visit her grandparents every summer. They lived in a house up the hill from us. This little girl's name was Nancy, and she loved to come to the store. When she did, she always called me Ricky. I told her a million times my name was Jackie, but to her it was always Ricky. It drove me crazy.

Finally my mother explained that Nancy had us confused with the Nelson family on TV. Mother was Harriet, my dad was Ozzie, my brother was David, and I was Ricky. Logical, I guess, but I still couldn't figure why I was the only one she called by the TV name.

Well, I guess life back then was like a sitcom of sorts. We certainly were as happy as any TV family at that time. Eventually, death and the dollar infringed upon this picture. The family faced a tragedy, and the store was torn down.

After my mother died and my father remarried, he and his new wife built a fine brick home on the site of the store. I don't think they ever realized they were building it on sacred ground.

Love Can Be Real at Any Age

Now that I have passed from the "thirty-something" group to the "forty-something" group, I have entered the age where the children of my contemporaries are teenagers. Whenever we parents gather, the talk is usually of kids and their problems, and our problems with their problems. Currently there has been a lot of talk about young love and how cute and fickle it is.

Having been a teenager at one time, I can remember love at that age being anything but cute and/or fickle. I don't know what happens to adults—when it comes to remembering what life was like back then, our brains seem to atrophy. But my vision of "love among the teens" is as clear now as it was back in the '50s and '60s.

I fell in love when I was 15. The object of my love was 13. It was not a fickle infatuation, but a relationship that lasted for five years. And when it was over, I thought I couldn't draw breath. Aside from the death of my mother, it was the most traumatic event in my life. I would hate for anybody to ever categorize the feelings I had for "the cheerleader" as anything but love.

When we first started dating, I had to have her home by 9:30. That gave us time to go to a movie and come straight back to her house. Eventually, the time was upped to 10, and then 11. Over a period of five years, parents do have to give a little.

For a relationship to end in such misery, it surely was good while it lasted. The cheerleader and I were as much a part of Clinton High School legend as any couple could be. We were perfect together. We had always gone together. We would always be together. Other couples might come and go, but Jackie and Elaine were permanent.

So what happened to forever? College did us in. I went away to college and left her to finish up her junior and senior years of high school. We had big plans. She would take a two-year business course in college, and that would have me finishing college when she got her business degree. Then she would work and send me to law school. We had our plans all made.

We did make it through the first two years of my being in college. But then she went off to start her business course, and she hated it. She wanted to quit school and get married. I wanted to wait until she got the two years finished. The only problem was that she had met a guy who didn't care if she could type—and he thought marriage sounded great.

I remember going to see Elaine in October of that year. I knew something was wrong from the minute I arrived. She didn't say anything right off, but finally she said she was going to take off THE RING. Now this was not a high school ring or a diamond ring or anything like that. This was a friendship ring I had given her for the first Valentine's Day we were together. It was not a ring made of gold. In truth, it had tarnished her finger. But she had never taken it off, never. That October she did.

We still saw each other off and on for a few months, and then things sort of slid away. Elaine got married the beginning of the next summer. That's when I had trouble breathing. It was as though my whole life was never, ever going to be happy again. And for a long time, it wasn't.

So I have no sympathy for parents who tell me about the silly little romances their teens are involved in. I had one of those "silly little romances," and it was as genuine an emotion as I have ever felt. There was nothing immature or foolish about it. Like the song says, "A kiss is still a kiss as time goes by."

My "teen" romance affected my life for years after Elaine and I broke up. BUT, I did finally get over her. And years later I fell in love again—and it was even better than what I had lost. But the feelings I found at 28 were no more valid than those I had felt at 16. Love comes to us at different ages—and whenever it arrives, it is real for that time and that place. Calendar years have nothing to do with feelings.

Surely you remember being a teenager. And you must remember being in love. This Valentine's Day, try to remember—for the sake of understanding your teen.

The Luge Was a Sport Created for Him

From the earliest days of my life, I can remember looking for "my" sport. Everybody I knew had one. Everyone was good at something. Everybody had one sport he loved. I didn't. I was always too clumsy, too uncoordinated, too hot, too tired, or too lazy. When God was handing out athletic ability and enthusiasm, I was out to lunch. Still, being a boy growing up in the South, I made an effort. Take baseball. I played Pee Wee League and Little League. I was on the team. I had a uniform.

My position was right field. That's the safest spot for any non-athlete to play. You can stand out there inning after inning and never come near a baseball. I loved it. It was the closest to non-playing that playing can get. Nobody except some wild left-handed hitter hits a ball into right field.

Still, I did have to bat. And somehow I always came up with two outs and hundreds of people on base. Other kids prayed for home runs; I prayed for a walk. If not that, I prayed, then let me get hit by the ball. I didn't get hit very often: but, thank the Lord, I did get walked a lot. Of course, that meant I had to figure out how to get from base to base. I rarely did.

In high school, I decided basketball was going to be my sport—rather, my two good friends, Chuck and Hollis, decided that for me. Easy for them—they were basketball aces who could ring baskets with their eyes closed.

One whole summer they worked with me to try to get me proficient at the game. I did get to where I could dribble the ball. I did get to where I could block a shot. I did get to where I could hit a foul shot. I just couldn't do more than one thing at a time. If I was concentrating on my dribbling, I couldn't shoot. If I blocked a shot and got the ball, I was too excited to dribble. So my dreams of basketball glory faded away, too.

Through the years I ran through tennis, volleyball, croquet, racquetball, handball, ping pong and horse-shoes—with mild successes sometimes; big successes never.

But the other day I discovered what my sport is. If I had discovered this sport in high school, I probably would have lettered. It's the sport I was created to excel in. It is called THE LUGE.

From what I understand of this wonderful sport, the more you weigh, the better you are at it. I could be as fat as a Sumo wrestler, and that would be just fine. There is no need to "get into shape," because with this sport, being "out" is being in. Bring on those munchies! I'm going into training!

The second best thing about it is that you do it lying down. You just get on your little Luge machine and let gravity take you around. There is no huffing and puffing, no straining of muscles. The less movement, the better, so that you will not upset your cart and slide onto the ice.

In my mind, I hear Calgary calling. But I must admit that I'm not yet ready for the Olympics. The year 1992 will have to be my year. By then, I will have my weight up—if

I really work on it, that is. And I will have the art of lying down on the job down to perfection.

So if you observe me getting bigger and lazier, don't be critical. I have found my sport. I have heard my calling. I am a Luge fanatic, and I am going for the gold!

Grass Is Greener in Your Own Yard

Every once in a while I get concerned about overpopulation. I decide that all of the land is being used up by buildings, and that we are all going to choke to death because there aren't enough trees and greenery to give back oxygen. I haven't learned enough to be concerned about the hole in the ozone layer, but I am sure that, sooner or later, that will also be a point of concern with me.

As I drive down the highway to work each morning, I can see the signs of more industry coming into my home county. For a month or more now, they have been working on a new access road to the interstate, and there is talk of a new bypass around the city of Perry. A few years ago, it would have been hilarious to talk about a road going around Perry to cut down on traffic.

But Houston County is booming, and that means more buildings, more concrete, more people. And that is what precipitated my claustrophobic concern. I could just see all of the land going faster and faster until it was all used up. After all, land is something they are not manufacturing more of in any way.

If I had lots and lots of money, I think I would invest in land. I would amass miles and miles of it and call it

"Cooperwood" or something equally grand. And when my sons grew up, they would get a plot for their homes where they could live with their wives and my grandchildren. It would be just like "Dallas" or "Bonanza."

Anyway, to get back to the point of this column, I had to go to St. Simons on business today, and I rode through the back roads of Georgia to get there. It had been a while since I had made this trip, and I had forgotten how much farmland you pass through. Enough land and trees are in this area alone to keep us safe for another hundred years or more.

It was also fascinating to see the little towns that look the way my hometown in South Carolina looked 10 years ago. Take away the modern cars and the newspaper vending machines, and you are back in the 1950s. Life is a little slower in these places, and the hustle of modern life is still kept at bay.

I wonder what it is like to live in places like that today. Do the people there worry about a high crime rate or drugs or alcohol abuse? Do their kids read books, rather than watch television for hours on end? Do the local churches worry about the health of their congregations rather than their wallets? Is life any simpler there?

Maybe one day I will find out. Maybe I will just move, lock, stock and barrel, to a place with a population of 500 or less. Maybe I will get back to the basics of nature.

Maybe I will learn to hunt and fish and plant a garden. Maybe I will learn to communicate with nature. Maybe I will learn to sleep under the stars . . . Er . . . maybe I'm just getting carried away. Maybe I will just stay where I am!

Teller Gave Him No Interest for His Money

Did you ever have one of those "I'm-getting-the-flu" days? You know, the kind where your head hurts, your eyes are running, and your throat is clogged? That's the way I felt last Monday, and sure enough, I came down with a super case of the flu. But before I became bedridden, I had another one of my little stress tests that will one day give me the big attack.

I have told people over and over it is not the mortgage nor the fear of failure nor the rise in taxes that will do me in. It is the little foibles of life that will get the old ticker headed for the last roundup. Some examples are: newspaper machines that take my money, motorists who don't drive as I want them to, and bank tellers who aren't courteous. That last one is the subject of this column. Let me quickly make a disclaimer that this negative report is not about all bank tellers, but only one rotten apple in particular.

Now banks as a whole are pleasant places to go. I guess if you're there to ask for a loan and are turned down, that isn't so great--but I am talking about the normal transactions of cashing checks, etc. Banks even advertise about being warm, comfortable places. They emphasize the respect you'll get at this or that institution. Those are their selling points, and they know it.

They realize, as we do too, that there really isn't much difference between one bank and another. If you don't like the people who work there, you certainly are not going to give them your business. That's why my run-in with the "mad teller" was so galling.

On this day, when the flu bug was starting his trip around my insides, I found myself on a different side of town than I needed to be in order to get some banking matters done. So I went to a branch of my bank that I usually do not frequent. I didn't use the drive-through window but went inside to make my transaction. The bank was empty of customers except for me. Ms. Teller gave me a cheery "Hello" and asked how she could help me.

My need was to have $175 taken from my savings account, $150 put in my checking account, and $25 given to me in cash—not exactly a transaction that would affect Wall Street! I explained what I needed and handed her my savings account book and my checkbook so she could get the proper account numbers.

Not batting a false eyelash, she slid them back to me. "I will need for you to fill out two slips to do that," she chirped. My head was wobbling, my eyes were blurring, my throat was constricting, "Couldn't you do it for me?" I asked. Fool that I was.

"No," she smiled again. "I prefer that you do it. If I make them out and there is an error, then it would be my fault. So it's better that you do it. The other week I did it for a lady, and there was some mistake, and it resulted in some bad checks."

Either my stubborn streak or the flu was making me hostile. "I thought this was a service of the bank," I muttered through clenched teeth.

"No. We prefer for the customer to fill out the forms," she said, holding firm. This was one determined woman. She thrust the slips at me again. "Just fill them out."

I stared at the two forms. They looked interchangeable. Which was which? One must be for savings and one must be for checking, but "Miss Helpful of 1988" hadn't offered a suggestion of designation.

The flu bug was screaming for release. The forms now appeared to be written in Greek. And the tacky teller was standing firm. There was to be no winning this war. So I surrendered. I pushed the forms back to her and told her quietly and politely (well, maybe not too quietly or politely) to forget it!

As I was walking out the door, I heard her say, "Well, I guess I could fill them out for you."

I didn't go back. Instead, I drove across town to my familiar, wonderful branch and saw my old friends. They were waiting to serve me with open arms and ready smiles. They asked what videos I had seen lately and what I thought of the weather. I told them about my flu symptoms, and they consoled me. And they handled my transactions without my doing anything but signing my name.

Wouldn't it be great if that non-helpful teller would read this and change her ways? But that won't happen. Even if she read it, she would be thinking it applied to someone else. That's always the case: the other guy is always the wrong one. We never see the faults within ourselves. Still, if there is justice left in this world, the uncooperative young woman did at least catch the flu from me!

Ben and Betty Battle Over Day Care

Just about everyone I know who is married is part of a two-career family. The days of the wife staying home and keeping house and raising the kids is gone with the wind. Oh, there are still a few cases here and there, but even in the Deep South, we've come a long way, baby. And the babies are the ones who are having to make do.

My friend the newspaper writer and his wife are now at the six-week period in the life of their son. Six weeks doesn't seem very old for a newborn, but that is generally accepted as the magic cut off time when the baby is packed off to day care, and momma goes back to work.

For my friends Ben and Betty, the thought of sending six-week-old Bob away for the day is fraught with peril. Bob doesn't seem to be concerned, but Betty is a wreck. In most cases it is harder on the mom than on the dad to ship the baby out to dubious day care. And in the case of my friends, Ben is the "heavy."

Ben has recited all the reasons day care should be used: (1) The kid needs to learn how to be with other children, (2) Betty needs to be out of the house, (3) Bob will be potty-trained quicker when he sees how tidy the other kids are, and (4) Bob and Betty need Betty's income.

Betty has an answer for it all: (1) Bob can hardly focus on his toes, much less look at other children; (2) Betty has learned to be happy in the house - it has become her world; (3) Bob can wear diapers until he is in third grade, and (4) if Ben was any kind of provider, they wouldn't need Betty's income.

As you can see, this war of the sexes can get pretty rough pretty quick. But necessities of life, or perceived necessities of life, work their power, and all over the country baby Bobs go off to day care centers.

In the case of Betty and Ben, they did handle the selection of the day care center in the best way. They visited every possible day care center in their town. They checked with the Chamber of Commerce and the Better Business Bureau to see if there had been any complaints. They physically checked out the accommodations. And most important, they asked if the staff was adverse to drop-in visits.

You would be surprised at how many places say they do not want surprise visits by parents. They say the children have to be prepared for the parents' coming by. They say surprise visits upset the children. They say nap times cannot be interrupted. I say, "Hogwash!" If I had my child in a day care center, I would make those surprise visits, just to see how the place is run when no parents are around.

My wife and I chose not to use day care when our children were smaller. We were financially able to do so, and I am grateful we were. Some of our closest friends did use day care, and their kids suffered no ill effects. There is good and bad in all things.

But one day we did have to put our son, JJ, in day care. I had a business meeting and Terry had a doctor's appointment. We could not find a sitter. So we went to a day care place. I was the one who took him, as Terry said it would traumatize her to leave him there.

When I got there, it was as though the floor was covered with babies. Now realize, this is how it was in my mind. I am sure there were not babies asleep on every spare inch of linoleum, but it seemed that way. And watching all of those thousands of babies was one poor, fragile lady. Again, that is how it seemed in my mind. I handed over my child as if I was consigning him to a fate worse than death. And I went to my meeting feeling like the worst father of the century.

Terry picked up JJ when her appointment was completed. He was happy, clean and smiling. He did not catch any diseases from the stay, and he was none the worse for wear. But from that point on, we used baby sitters when we had to be out. My imagination had been too fertile, and a totally innocent experience had scared me.

Whether you use day care is your choice. There are some excellent places, and some not so excellent. The important thing is that you check them out thoroughly and feel satisfied you have made the best choice. Then perhaps you can rest a little easier after you drop off your child.

Betty and Ben send Bob off to day care next week. With a little luck and a lot of hope, Bob will be fine. And with a little more hope and faith, so will Betty and Ben.

Revenge Can Be Sweet

Spring is probably my favorite season of the year. Winter is just too dreary, fall is when everything is dying, and summer is hot, and I hate to sweat. So that leaves spring, the season of life and renewal. The time of rebirth and continued life. It's my kind of time.

Spring is the time for hope. Whenever anyone has been sick and I have been concerned about them, I have always thought that if they could make it through the winter and last into spring they would be all right. Just like O'Henry's "The Last Leaf," I thought spring was a talisman to cling to until the illness had passed.

But being such a great season, spring has to have its drawbacks. One of these is the masochistic ritual of class reunions. Just about everyone I know went to high school or college with somebody they hated. I don't mean they disliked this person—no, no, they hated them. And no matter how many years pass, that detested person still has the capacity to bring up anger, rejection or feelings of doubt.

Maybe you were perfect and didn't feel that way about anyone, but not me. There was one guy at college that I loathed. He was one of the meanest people I ever met. He probably drowned puppies for a pastime. I never felt his wrath or his anger directly, because I was not important enough for him to harass.

Still, I saw how he treated other people. There was this one poor girl who was crazy about him—why she was, I'll never know. He joked about her to all of his friends, and I know she heard about what he said.

One time he took her out and had a tape recorder in the back seat of his car. When the date was over, he brought the tape into the dorm and played it for the pleasure of his hall buddies. I think that was the final straw for the girl. When she heard about it, she left the school – went home for the weekend and just never came back.

The only thing this guy did like was his car. It was his pride and joy. He waxed it, polished it, babied it, l-o-o-oved it. It purred when he drove it, and he purred when he drove it. It was a perfect matching of man and machine, especially when it was low on fuel. He was about empty on character, and the car was about empty on gas.

My roommate in college was president of the student body. Stewart was a good, conscientious student. He never got into trouble. He never even thought about getting into trouble. Well, the only time he ever got into trouble was when he listened to me. And he listened to me complain constantly about this pain-in-the-neck guy.

Others must have been feeling the same way, because word up and down the halls of our dorm was that something was going to happen. It was not a question of if, it was a question of when, what and how. Finally, the word came around through the grapevine that it was going to happen to "the car."

The car was always parked in the same spot behind the dorm. It was a spot isolated, away from the other cars so there would be no possibility of its getting scratched. It had a tarpaulin covering it so the dew would not dampen nor the sun rot.

The attack on the car took place in the middle of the night and was carried out by a group called "The Midnight Men." They sneaked out to the victim's vehicle and undid all the lug nuts on the tires so that when the car was driven, it would drop.

The next morning, we stationed ourselves next to our window. From that vantage point, we could see "the car." Finally, Mr. No-Character raced from the door of the dorm. He carefully removed the cover of the car. Folded it neatly and put it in the back seat. Picked some lint from off the hood. Then settled himself into the car and started it.

No tires fell off. We were stunned. He put the car in reverse and started backwards. No tires even trembled. It took all of my willpower not to curse the stupid tires from my window.

The car backed up, and then it started forward. There was a trembling, a shake, sort of a sigh, and then the tires began to wobble and move. The vehicle was still in drive and picking up speed when the first one collapsed. And then the entire car collapsed. It hit the ground with a screeching thud.

The deed was done. "The Midnight Men" had completed their mission. And they were never discovered. There were a lot of threats from the administration and from the victim himself, but no one was ever implicated. The victim screamed that the administration wasn't trying to find out who did it, and maybe they weren't. Maybe they, too, knew what a rotten person he was. He screamed even louder when he got a note in the mail that said, "One broken car equals one broken heart. This was for Maryanne. Signed –The Midnight Men."

The car was, of course, repaired, but it never drove quite right after that. It had some squeaks and groans that he could never eliminate. His friends said he never felt the same about the car again.

Did this incident change his attitude on life? No. He graduated, went into business and is reputed to be one of the most ruthless, unpleasant, successful people in South Carolina today. He has had three wives and numerous employees. He fires spouses and workers with equal skill.

When our college reunion comes along, I know he will be there. The worst ones always come back. My stomach will churn, but I won't say anything. But Stewart is going to be there this year, too, and the BMW our old adversary now loves might be getting a little wobbly before the weekend is over.

The Midnight Men may also come back to that reunion.

Don't Settle for Ordinary

The best gift my parents ever gave me was the ability to dream. I was told from the earliest age that I was special, and that I could be anything I wanted to be. The great thing was that I believed them. I have always felt I could do anything I really put my mind to doing.

Now since I am not President of the United States, reality had to sink in somewhere. But the truth is I never wanted to be President. What I wanted to do was write. And that takes a degree of talent. The question then became did I have the talent. That's when the doubts came in. I was special, I was smart, but did I have talent.

Even when we put on the show of being supremely confident, each of us down deep has some doubts. Those doubts are what usually defeat us. Whether we have talent or not, most of us never make the effort to find out.

The best gift my wife ever gave me was the right to fail. She didn't wrap that present up in a package and hand it to me. I don't even remember the day that I became aware she had given me the gift. But one day it was there. I had a person who would still love me no matter what I did or how silly I looked.

That presence of faith and support made it possible for me to try to write. How it gave her the ability to keep a straight face when reading some of my earlier efforts, I don't know. But I knew she thought I could do it, and more importantly, that if I tried and failed that would be all right too.

During the early days of my writing I got some criticism that would knock Hemingway off his heels. I remember submitting an effort to an editor who told me he wouldn't wrap his garbage in trash like that. I took my trash out of his hands and went on my way. Three editors down the line from that guy bought it.

As my friends all know, I haven't won the Pulitzer Prize — yet. Maybe I never will, but then again maybe I will. The exciting thing is you never know. Anything is possible if you try.

I see kids lock themselves into careers or marriages just because they think they can't achieve or are not suited for anything else. We sell ourselves and them short every day. We tell them to look for the superficial instead of the deep. We tell them to look for the money and ignore the cause. We tell them to settle for second best because best is out of their reach.

Still some of them do get the message they can achieve greatness. Some get the message they can find true love. Some get the message that they can take that extra step and make a difference. They learn to "dream the impossible dream" or to "wish upon a star."

All of the great songs, movies and books push the theme of being more than we think we are. Still, too many of us brush that off as Madison Avenue pipe dreams. But it isn't so. I have heard so many times how we use only a fraction of our brain power during our lives. And when we are dead our heads are dead, and all that brain power is wasted.

So tell yourself you can do that secret wish you have inside you. Dream some dreams that might challenge your life. Don't just settle for the ordinary when the extraordinary might be only one step away. Failures are no fun, but they generally are not fatal. If you believe in yourself, you can survive them. You may not reach the unreachable star, but striving to get there is a heck of a lot more fun that settling for the safety net.

Feeling special and being unafraid of failure are two of the greatest gifts you can get. Give them to yourself and to someone you love.

Epilogue

Each day the journey continues. Some days I am on rough roads and at other times on smooth. What is most worrisome is the fact that people are dropping out of the journey – and I miss them. As I was finishing this book, I received word that my best friend from childhood had died. He is called Chuck in this book, but his full name was Charles Reginald Tucker. He and I were born in the same month, the same year, in the same town. I can't remember ever not knowing him.

We went to grammar school, high school and college together. I was a member of the wedding party when he married his first wife, and he was in mine when I married my only wife. At the time of my marriage he noted the age difference between us and declared that he gave it a year at most. That was Tucker, he said what he thought.

For the last few years we hadn't seen too much of each other. He was busy with his life, and I was busy with mine. Still, every now and then the phone would ring, and it would be him. He would expound on what he thought of the latest political situations; reflect on how good the good old days were; tell me a few slightly off-color jokes; and then harass me for never being the one to call him.

Now he is gone, and like they always say – too late – I wish I had seen him more, talked to him more. He was my childhood friend and had memories of me that no one else had. Losing him is like skidding on ice. It makes for some uncertain times.

Still, the door is open and the road stretches ahead. There is more life to be lived, more lessons to be learned. The journey is not over. Tomorrow has not been lived.

JACKIE K. COOPER
Perry, Georgia
May 31, 1999